Keras Deep Learning Cookbook

Over 30 recipes for implementing deep neural networks
in Python

Rajdeep Dua
Manpreet Singh Ghotra

Keras Deep Learning Cookbook

Commissioning Editor: Amey Varangaonkar
Acquisition Editor: Karan Jain
Content Development Editor: Karan Thakkar
Technical Editor: Sagar Sawant
Copy Editor: Safis Editing
Project Coordinator: Nidhi Joshi
Proofreader: Safis Editing
Indexer: Pratik Shirodkar
Graphics: Jisha Chirayil
Production Coordinator: Aparna Bhagat

First published: October 2018

Production reference: 1301018

Published by Packt Publishing Ltd.
Livery Place
35 Livery Street
Birmingham
B3 2PB, UK.

ISBN 978-1-78862-175-5

www.packtpub.com

mapt.io

Mapt is an online digital library that gives you full access to over 5,000 books and videos, as well as industry leading tools to help you plan your personal development and advance your career. For more information, please visit our website.

Why subscribe?

- Spend less time learning and more time coding with practical eBooks and Videos from over 4,000 industry professionals

- Improve your learning with Skill Plans built especially for you

- Get a free eBook or video every month

- Mapt is fully searchable

- Copy and paste, print, and bookmark content

Packt.com

Did you know that Packt offers eBook versions of every book published, with PDF and ePub files available? You can upgrade to the eBook version at www.packt.com and as a print book customer, you are entitled to a discount on the eBook copy. Get in touch with us at customercare@packtpub.com for more details.

At www.packt.com, you can also read a collection of free technical articles, sign up for a range of free newsletters, and receive exclusive discounts and offers on Packt books and eBooks.

Contributors

About the authors

Rajdeep Dua has over 18 years experience in the cloud and big data space. He has taught Spark and big data at some of the most prestigious tech schools in India: IIIT Hyderabad, ISB, IIIT Delhi, and Pune College of Engineering. He currently leads the developer relations team at Salesforce India. He has also presented BigQuery and Google App Engine at the W3C conference in Hyderabad. He led the developer relations teams at Google, VMware, and Microsoft, and has spoken at hundreds of other conferences on the cloud. Some of the other references to his work can be seen at Your Story and on ACM digital library. His contributions to the open source community relate to Docker, Kubernetes, Android, OpenStack, and Cloud Foundry.

Manpreet Singh Ghotra has more than 15 years experience in software development for both enterprise and big data software. He is currently working at Salesforce on developing a machine learning platform/APIs using open source libraries and frameworks such as Keras, Apache Spark, and TensorFlow. He has worked on various machine learning systems, including sentiment analysis, spam detection, and anomaly detection. He was part of the machine learning group at one of the largest online retailers in the world, working on transit time calculations using Apache Mahout, and the R recommendation system, again using Apache Mahout. With a master's and postgraduate degree in machine learning, he has contributed to, and worked for, the machine learning community.

About the reviewer

Sujit Pal works at Elsevier Labs, a research and development group within the Reed-Elsevier PLC Group. His interests are in information retrieval, distributed processing, ontology development, natural language processing, and machine learning, and codes in Python, Scala, and Java. He combines his skills in these areas in order to help build new features or feature improvements in different products across the company. He believes in lifelong learning and blogs about his experiences at `sujitpal.blogspot.com`.

Packt is searching for authors like you

If you're interested in becoming an author for Packt, please visit `authors.packtpub.com` and apply today. We have worked with thousands of developers and tech professionals, just like you, to help them share their insight with the global tech community. You can make a general application, apply for a specific hot topic that we are recruiting an author for, or submit your own idea.

Table of Contents

Preface

Keras has quickly emerged as a popular deep learning library. Written in Python, it allows you to train convolutional as well as recurrent neural networks with speed and accuracy.

The *Keras Deep Learning Cookbook* shows you how to tackle different problems encountered while training efficient deep learning models, with the help of the popular Keras library. This book covers installing and setting up Keras, while also demonstrating how you can perform deep learning with Keras in the TensorFlow, Apache MXNet, and CNTK backends.

From loading data to fitting and evaluating your model for optimal performance, you will work through a step-by-step process to tackle every possible problem faced while training deep models. You will implement convolutional and recurrent neural networks, adversarial networks, and more with the help of this handy guide. In addition to this, you will learn how to train these models for real-world image and language processing tasks.

By the end of this book, you will have a practical, hands-on understanding of how you can leverage the power of Python and Keras to perform effective deep learning.

Who this book is for

Keras Deep Learning Cookbook is for you if you are a data scientist or machine learning expert who wants to find practical solutions to common problems encountered while training deep learning models. A basic understanding of Python and some experience in machine learning and neural networks is required for this book.

What this book covers

Chapter 1, *Keras Installation*, covers various installation and setup procedures, as well as defining various Keras configurations.

Chapter 2, *Working with Keras Datasets and Models*, covers using various datasets, such as CIFAR10, CIFAR100, or MNIST, and many other datasets and models used for image classification.

Chapter 3, *Data Preprocessing, Optimization, and Visualization*, covers various preprocessing and optimization techniques using Keras. The optimization techniques covered include TFOptimizer, AdaDelta, and many more.

`Chapter 4`, *Classification Using Different Keras Layers*, details various Keras layers, for example, recurrent layers, and convolutional layers.

`Chapter 5`, *Implementing Convolutional Neural Networks*, teaches you convolutional neural network algorithms in detail, using the example of cervical cancer classification and the digit recognition dataset.

`Chapter 6`, *Generative Adversarial Networks*, covers basic generative adversarial networks (GANs) and boundary-seeking GAN.

`Chapter 7`, *Recurrent Neural Networks*, covers the basics of recurrent neural networks in order to implement Keras based on historical datasets.

`Chapter 8`, *Natural Language Processing Using Keras Models*, covers the basics of NLP for word analysis and sentiment analysis using Keras.

`Chapter 9`, *Text Summarization Using Keras Models*, shows you how to use Keras models for text summarization when using the Amazon reviews dataset.

`Chapter 10`, *Reinforcement Learning*, focuses on formulating and developing reinforcement learning models using Keras.

To get the most out of this book

Readers should have some basic knowledge of Keras and deep learning.

Download the example code files

You can download the example code files for this book from your account at `www.packt.com`. If you purchased this book elsewhere, you can visit `www.packt.com/support` and register to have the files emailed directly to you.

You can download the code files by following these steps:

1. Log in or register at `www.packt.com`.
2. Select the **SUPPORT** tab.
3. Click on **Code Downloads & Errata**.
4. Enter the name of the book in the **Search** box and follow the onscreen instructions.

Once the file is downloaded, please make sure that you unzip or extract the folder using the latest version of:

- WinRAR/7-Zip for Windows
- Zipeg/iZip/UnRarX for Mac
- 7-Zip/PeaZip for Linux

The code bundle for the book is also hosted on GitHub at `https://github.com/PacktPublishing/Keras-Deep-Learning-Cookbook`. In case there's an update to the code, it will be updated on the existing GitHub repository.

We also have other code bundles from our rich catalog of books and videos available at `https://github.com/PacktPublishing/`. Check them out!

Download the color images

We also provide a PDF file that has color images of the screenshots/diagrams used in this book. You can download it here: `http://www.packtpub.com/sites/default/files/downloads/9781788621755_ColorImages.pdf`.

Conventions used

There are a number of text conventions used throughout this book.

`CodeInText`: Indicates code words in text, database table names, folder names, filenames, file extensions, pathnames, dummy URLs, user input, and Twitter handles. Here is an example: "Finally, we save all the reviews into a `pickle` file."

A block of code is set as follows:

```
stories = list()
for i, text in enumerate(clean_texts):
    stories.append({'story': text, 'highlights': clean_summaries[i]})
```

When we wish to draw your attention to a particular part of a code block, the relevant lines or items are set in bold:

```
from keras.datasets import cifar10
```

Any command-line input or output is written as follows:

```
sudo apt-get install graphviz
```

Bold: Indicates a new term, an important word, or words that you see on screen. For example, words in menus or dialog boxes appear in the text like this. Here is an example: "Choose the appropriate instance type: **g3.4xlarge**."

Warnings or important notes appear like this.

Tips and tricks appear like this.

Sections

In this book, you will find several headings that appear frequently (*Getting ready*, *How to do it...*, *How it works...*, *There's more...*, and *See also*).

To give clear instructions on how to complete a recipe, use these sections as follows:

Getting ready

This section tells you what to expect in the recipe and describes how to set up any software or any preliminary settings required for the recipe.

How to do it...

This section contains the steps required to follow the recipe.

How it works...

This section usually consists of a detailed explanation of what happened in the previous section.

There's more...

This section consists of additional information about the recipe in order to make you more knowledgeable about the recipe.

See also

This section provides helpful links to other useful information for the recipe.

Get in touch

Feedback from our readers is always welcome.

General feedback: If you have questions about any aspect of this book, mention the book title in the subject of your message and email us at `customercare@packtpub.com`.

Errata: Although we have taken every care to ensure the accuracy of our content, mistakes do happen. If you have found a mistake in this book, we would be grateful if you would report this to us. Please visit `www.packt.com/submit-errata`, selecting your book, clicking on the Errata Submission Form link, and entering the details.

Piracy: If you come across any illegal copies of our works in any form on the internet, we would be grateful if you would provide us with the location address or website name. Please contact us at `copyright@packt.com` with a link to the material.

If you are interested in becoming an author: If there is a topic that you have expertise in, and you are interested in either writing or contributing to a book, please visit `authors.packtpub.com`.

Reviews

Please leave a review. Once you have read and used this book, why not leave a review on the site that you purchased it from? Potential readers can then see and use your unbiased opinion to make purchase decisions, we at Packt can understand what you think about our products, and our authors can see your feedback on their book. Thank you!

For more information about Packt, please visit `packt.com`.

1
Keras Installation

In this chapter, we will cover the following recipes:

- Installing Keras on Ubuntu 16.04
- Installing Keras with Jupyter Notebook in a Docker image
- Installing Keras on Ubuntu 16.04 with GPU enabled

Introduction

In this chapter, we look at how Keras can be installed on Ubuntu and CentOS. We will use Ubuntu 16.04, 64-bit (Canonical, Ubuntu, 16.04 LTS, and amd64 xenial image build on 2017-10-26) for the installation.

Installing Keras on Ubuntu 16.04

Before installing Keras, we have to install the Theano and TensorFlow packages and their dependencies. Since it is a fresh OS, make sure Python is installed. Let's look at the following section for Python installation.

 Conda is an open source package management system and environment management system that runs on multiple OSes: Windows, macOS, and Linux. Conda installs, runs, and updates packages and their dependencies. Conda creates, saves, loads, and switches between environments on a local computer. It has been created for Python environments.

Getting ready

First you need to make sure you have a blank Ubuntu 16.04 OS locally or remotely available in the cloud and with root access.

How to do it...

In the following sections, we take a at the installation of each component that needs to be done before we can go ahead with the installation of Keras.

Installing miniconda

Before we proceed further, let's install `miniconda` to install the rest of the packages. Miniconda is a smaller version of the `conda` package manager. Python is bundled along with `miniconda`.

 It is recommended that users choose either Python 2.7 or Python 3.4. Python = 2.7* or (>= 3.4 and < 3.6). The Python development package (`python-dev` or `python-devel` on most Linux distributions) is recommended. We will focus on Python 2.7.

1. To install `miniconda`, let's first download the `sh` installer from the `continuum` repository:

```
wget
https://repo.continuum.io/miniconda/Miniconda2-latest-Linux-x86_64.
sh
chmod 755 Miniconda2-latest-Linux-x86_64.sh
./Miniconda2-latest-Linux-x86_64.sh
```

2. Once `conda` has been installed, we can use it to install the dependencies of Theano, TensorFlow, and Keras.

Installing numpy and scipy

The `numpy` and `scipy` packages are prerequisites for Theano installation. The following versions are recommended:

- NumPy >= 1.9.1 <= 1.12
- SciPy >= 0.14 < 0.17.1: Highly recommended for sparse matrix and support for special functions in Theano, SciPy >=0.8 would do the work

- BLAS installation (with Level 3 functionality) the recommended: MKL, this is free through `conda` with the `mkl-service` package

Basic Linear Algebra Subprograms (BLAS) is a specification that defines a set of low-level routines for performing common linear algebra operations such as vector addition, scalar multiplication, dot products, linear combinations, and matrix multiplication. These are the de facto standard low-level routines for linear algebra libraries; the routines have bindings for both C and Fortran. Level 3 is referred to as matrix -to-matrix multiplications.

1. Execute the following command to install `numpy` and `scipy`. (Make sure `conda` is in your `PATH`):

```
conda install numpy
conda install scipy
```

The output of the `scipy` installation is shown as follows. Notice that it installs `libgfortran` as part of the `scipy` installation:

```
Fetching package metadata ..........
Solving package specifications: .
Package plan for installation in environment
/home/ubuntu/miniconda2:
```

2. The following new packages will also be installed:

```
libgfortran-ng: 7.2.0-h9f7466a_2
scipy: 1.0.0-py27hf5f0f52_0
Proceed ([y]/n)?
libgfortran-ng 100%
|#########################################################|
Time: 0:00:00 36.60 MB/s
scipy-1.0.0-py 100%
|#########################################################|
Time: 0:00:00 66.62 MB/s
```

Installing mkl

1. `mkl` is a math library for Intel and compatible processors. It is a part of `numpy`, but we want to make sure it is installed before we install Theano and TensorFlow:

```
conda install mkl
```

The output of the installation is given as follows. In our case, `miniconda2` has already installed the latest version of `mkl`:

```
Fetching package metadata ..........
Solving package specifications: .
# All requested packages already installed.
# packages in environment at /home/ubuntu/miniconda2:
#
mkl 2018.0.1 h19d6760_4
```

2. Once all the prerequisites are installed, let's install TensorFlow.

Installing TensorFlow

1. Execute the following command to install `tensorflow` using `conda`:

```
conda install -c conda-forge tensorflow
```

The output of this command will fetch metadata and install a list of packages, as follows:

```
Fetching package metadata ............
Solving package specifications: .
Package plan for installation in environment
/home/ubuntu/miniconda2:
```

2. The following new packages will also be installed:

```
bleach: 1.5.0-py27_0 conda-forge
funcsigs: 1.0.2-py_2 conda-forge
futures: 3.2.0-py27_0 conda-forge
html5lib: 0.9999999-py27_0 conda-forge
markdown: 2.6.9-py27_0 conda-forge
mock: 2.0.0-py27_0 conda-forge
pbr: 3.1.1-py27_0 conda-forge
protobuf: 3.5.0-py27_0 conda-forge
tensorboard: 0.4.0rc3-py27_0 conda-forge
tensorflow: 1.4.0-py27_0 conda-forge
webencodings: 0.5-py27_0 conda-forge
werkzeug: 0.12.2-py_1 conda-forge
```

3. A higher-priority channel will supersede the following packages, as follows:

```
conda: 4.3.30-py27h6ae6dc7_0 --> 4.3.29-py27_0 conda-forge
conda-env: 2.6.0-h36134e3_1 --> 2.6.0-0 conda-forge
Proceed ([y]/n)? y
```

```
conda-env-2.6. 100%
|############################################################|
Time: 0:00:00 1.67 MB/s
...
mock-2.0.0-py2 100%
|############################################################|
Time: 0:00:00 26.00 MB/s
conda-4.3.29-p 100%
|############################################################|
Time: 0:00:00 27.46 MB/s
```

4. Once TensorFlow has been installed, let's test it with a simple program. Create a new file called `hello_tf.py` with the following command:

   ```
   vi hello_tf.py
   ```

5. Add the following code to this file and save the file:

   ```
   import tensorflow as tf
   hello = tf.constant('Greetings, TensorFlow!')
   sess = tf.Session()
   print(sess.run(hello))
   ```

6. Execute the file created from the command line:

   ```
   python hello_tf.py
   ```

   The output will make sure the library has been successfully installed:

   ```
   Greetings, TensorFlow!
   ```

Installing Keras

`conda-forge` is a GitHub entity with a repository of `conda` recipes.

1. Next, we will install Keras using `conda` from `conda-forge`
2. Execute the following command on the Terminal:

   ```
   conda install -c conda-forge keras
   ```

The following listed output will confirm that Keras is installed:

```
Fetching package metadata .............
Solving package specifications: .
Package plan for installation in environment
/home/ubuntu/miniconda2:
```

The following new packages will also be installed:

```
h5py: 2.7.1-py27_2 conda-forge
hdf5: 1.10.1-1 conda-forge
keras: 2.0.9-py27_0 conda-forge
libgfortran: 3.0.0-1
pyyaml: 3.12-py27_1 conda-forge
Proceed ([y]/n)? y
libgfortran-3. 100%
|###########################################################|
Time: 0:00:00 35.16 MB/s
hdf5-1.10.1-1. 100%
|###########################################################|
Time: 0:00:00 34.26 MB/s
pyyaml-3.12-py 100%
|###########################################################|
Time: 0:00:00 60.08 MB/s
h5py-2.7.1-py2 100%
|###########################################################|
Time: 0:00:00 58.54 MB/s
keras-2.0.9-py 100%
|###########################################################|
Time: 0:00:00 45.92 MB/s
```

3. Let's verify the Keras installation with the following code:

```
$ python
Python 2.7.14 |Anaconda, Inc.| (default, Oct 16 2017, 17:29:19)
```

4. Execute the following command to verify that Keras has been installed:

```
> from keras.models import Sequential
Using TensorFlow backend.
>>>
```

Notice that Keras is using the TensorFlow backend.

Using the Theano backend with Keras

1. Let's modify the default configuration and change TensorFlow to Theano as the backend of Keras. Modify the `keras.json` file:

   vi .keras/keras.json

   The default file has the following content:

   ```
   { "image_data_format": "channels_last",
     "epsilon": 1e-07,
     "floatx": "float32",
     "backend": "tensorflow"
   }
   ```

2. The modified file will look like the following file. The `"backend"` value has been changed to `"theano"`:

   ```
   { "image_data_format": "channels_last",
     "epsilon": 1e-07,
     "floatx": "float32",
     "backend": "theano"
   }
   ```

3. Run the Python console and import `Sequential` from `keras.model` using the Theano backend:

   ```
   $ python
   Python 2.7.14 |Anaconda, Inc.| (default, Oct 16 2017, 17:29:19)
   [GCC 7.2.0] on linux2
   Type "help", "copyright", "credits" or "license" for more
   information.
   >>> from keras.models import Sequential
   ```

Notice how the backend has changed to Theano.

We have installed `miniconda`, all the dependencies of TensorFlow, and Theano. This was followed by installing TensorFlow and Theano itself. Finally, we installed Keras. We also learned how to change the backend of Keras from TensorFlow to Theano.

Installing Keras with Jupyter Notebook in a Docker image

In this recipe, we learn how to install and use a Docker container running Keras inside a container and access it using Jupyter.

Getting ready

Install the latest version of the Docker CLI from `https://docs.docker.com/engine/installation/`.

How to do it...

In the following section, we will be learning how to install the Docker container.

Installing the Docker container

1. Execute the following command on the Terminal to run the container. The container image is available with the tag `rajdeepd/jupyter-keras`:

```
docker run -d -p 8888:8888 rajdeepd/jupyter-keras start-notebook.sh
--NotebookApp.token=''
```

2. This will install the Notebook locally and start it as well. You can execute the `docker ps -a` command and see the output in the Terminal, as follows:

```
CONTAINER ID          IMAGE                     COMMAND
CREATED               STATUS                    PORTS
NAMES
45998a5eea89          rajdeepd/jupyter-keras    "tini -- start-
not..."                About an hour ago Up About an hour
0.0.0.0:8888->8888/tcp    admiring_wing
```

Please note that the host port of `8888` is mapped to the container port of `8888`.

3. Open the browser at the following URL `http://localhost:8888`:

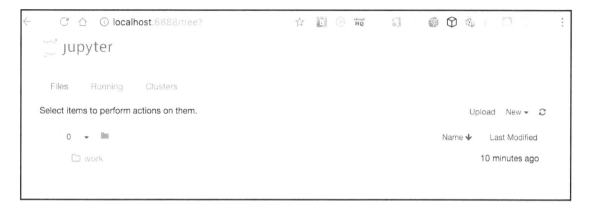

You will notice that Jupyter is running. You can create a new Notebook and run Keras-specific code.

Installing the Docker container with the host volume mapped

In this section, we look at how to map the local volume `$(pwd)/keras-samples` to the work directory in the container.

1. Execute the `note -v flag` command, which does the volume mapping:

```
docker run -d -v /$(pwd)/keras-samples:/home/jovyan/work \
 -p 8888:8888 rajdeepd/jupyter-keras start-notebook.sh --
NotebookApp.token=''
```

If you go to the URL, you will notice the sample page being displayed.

2. If you got `/$(pwd)/keras-samples`, you will notice that the Notebooks are available in the `host` directory, and they also can be seen being loaded by Jupyter:

```
rdua1-ltm:keras-samples rdua$ pwd
 /Users/rdua/personal/keras-samples
 rdua1-ltm:keras-samples rdua$ ls
 MNIST CNN.ipynb sample_one.ipynb
```

If you open `MNIST CNN.ipynb`, it is a Keras CNN sample, which we will learn more about in the subsequent chapters.

In this recipe, we used the Docker image `rajdeepd/jupyter-keras` to create a Keras environment and access it from Jupyter running in the host environment.

Installing Keras on Ubuntu 16.04 with GPU enabled

In this recipe, we will install Keras on Ubuntu 16.04 with NVIDIA GPU enabled.

Getting ready

We are going to launch a GPU-enabled AWS EC2 instance and prepare it for the installed TensorFlow with the GPU and Keras. Launch the following AMI: **Ubuntu Server 16.04 LTS (HVM), SSD Volume Type - ami-aa2ea6d0**:

This is an AMI with Ubuntu 16.04 64 bit pre-installed, and it has the SSD volume type.

Choose the appropriate instance type: **g3.4xlarge**:

Once the VM is launched, assign the appropriate key that you will use to SSH into it. In our case, we used a pre-existing key:

SSH into the instance:

```
ssh -i aws/rd_app.pem ubuntu@34.201.110.131
```

How to do it...

1. Run the following commands to `update` and `upgrade` the OS:

```
sudo apt-get update
sudo apt-get upgrade
```

2. Install the `gcc` compiler and make the tool:

```
sudo apt install gcc
sudo apt install make
```

Installing cuda

1. Execute the following command to execute `cuda`:

   ```
   sudo apt-get install -y cuda
   ```

2. Check that `cuda` is installed and run a basic program:

   ```
   ls /usr/local/cuda-8.0
   bin extras lib64 libnvvp nvml README share targets version.txt
   doc include libnsight LICENSE nvvm samples src tools
   ```

3. Let's run one of the `cuda` samples after compiling it locally:

   ```
   export PATH=/usr/local/cuda-8.0/bin${PATH:+:${PATH}}
   export
   LD_LIBRARY_PATH=/usr/local/cuda-8.0/lib64\${LD_LIBRARY_PATH:+:${LD_
   LIBRARY_PATH}}
   cd /usr/local/cuda-8.0/samples/5_Simulations/nbody
   ```

4. Compile the sample and run it as follows:

   ```
   sudo make
   ```

   ```
   ./nbody
   ```

   You will see output similar to the following listing:

   ```
   Run "nbody -benchmark [-numbodies=<numBodies>]" to measure
   performance.
    -fullscreen (run n-body simulation in fullscreen mode)
    -fp64 (use double precision floating point values for simulation)
    -hostmem (stores simulation data in host memory)
    -benchmark (run benchmark to measure performance)
    -numbodies=<N> (number of bodies (>= 1) to run in simulation)
    -device=<d> (where d=0,1,2.... for the CUDA device to use)
    -numdevices=<i> (where i=(number of CUDA devices > 0) to use for
   simulation)
    -compare (compares simulation results running once on the default
   GPU and once on the CPU)
    -cpu (run n-body simulation on the CPU)
    -tipsy=<file.bin> (load a tipsy model file for simulation)
   ```

5. Next we install `cudnn`, which is a deep learning library from NVIDIA. You can find more information at `https://developer.nvidia.com/cudnn`.

Installing cudnn

1. Download cudnn from the NVIDIA site (https://developer.nvidia.com/rdp/assets/cudnn-8.0-linux-x64-v5.0-ga-tgz) and decompress the binary:

 Please note, you will need an NVIDIA developer account.

```
tar xvf cudnn-8.0-linux-x64-v5.1.tgz
```

We obtain the following output after decompressing the .tgz file:

```
cuda/include/cudnn.h
cuda/lib64/libcudnn.so
cuda/lib64/libcudnn.so.5
cuda/lib64/libcudnn.so.5.1.10
cuda/lib64/libcudnn_static.a
```

2. Copy these files to the /usr/local folder, as follows:

```
sudo cp cuda/include/cudnn.h /usr/local/cuda/include
sudo cp cuda/lib64/libcudnn* /usr/local/cuda/lib64

sudo chmod a+r /usr/local/cuda/include/cudnn.h
/usr/local/cuda/lib64/libcudnn*
```

Installing NVIDIA CUDA profiler tools interface development files

Install the NVIDIA CUDA profiler tools interface development files that are needed for TensorFlow GPU installation with the following code:

```
sudo apt-get install libcupti-dev
```

Installing the TensorFlow GPU version

Execute the following command to install the TensorFlow GPU version:

```
sudo pip install tensorflow-gpu
```

Installing Keras

For Keras, use the sample command, as used for the installation with GPUs:

```
sudo pip install keras
```

In this recipe, we learned how to install Keras on top of the TensorFlow GPU hooked to cuDNN and CUDA.

2
Working with Keras Datasets and Models

In this chapter, we will cover the following recipes:

- CIFAR-10 dataset
- CIFAR-100 dataset
- MNIST dataset
- Load data from a CSV file
- Models in Keras - getting started
- Sequential models
- Shared layer models
- Keras functional APIs
- Keras functional APIs - linking the layers
- Image classification using Keras functional APIs

Introduction

In this chapter, we will explore various datasets available by default in Keras and how to load and use them.

CIFAR-10 dataset

Load the CIFAR-10 small images classification dataset from `https://www.cs.toronto.edu/~kriz/cifar-10-python.tar.gz`. The CIFAR-10 dataset is made up of 60,000 32 x 32 color images in 10 classes, and there are 6000 images per class. The dataset consists of 50,000 training images and 10,000 test images.

The dataset has been divided into five training batches and one test batch, each with 10,000 images. The test batch contains 1,000 randomly selected images from each class. The training batches contain the rest of the images in a random order; some training batches may contain more images from one class than another. The training batches contain 5,000 images from each class, such as shown in the following image:

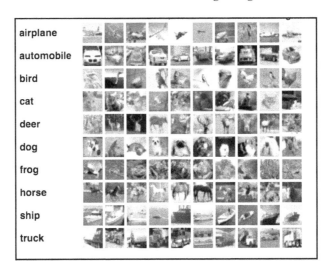

Reference: https://www.cs.toronto.edu/~kriz/cifar.html.

How to do it...

Let's load this dataset using the Keras APIs and print the shape and size:

```
from keras.datasets import cifar10

(X_train, y_train), (X_test, y_test) = cifar10.load_data()
print("X_train shape: " + str(X_train.shape))
print(y_train.shape)
print(X_test.shape)
print(y_test.shape)
```

The first time, it will download the file from the preceding site:

```
Downloading data from
https://www.cs.toronto.edu/~kriz/cifar-10-python.tar.gz
8192/170498071 [..............................] - ETA: 22:43
40960/170498071 [..............................] - ETA: 9:12
106496/170498071 [..............................] - ETA: 5:27
```

```
237568/170498071 [..............................] - ETA: 3:11
286720/170498071 [..............................] - ETA: 4:39
...
170418176/170498071 [==============================>.] - ETA: 0s
170467328/170498071 [==============================>.] - ETA: 0s
170500096/170498071 [==============================] - 308s 2us/step
```

The following output shows X_train has 50,000 images of size 32 x 32 containing three channels. y_train has 50,000 rows and one column with the image label. X_test and y_test also have a similar shape for 10,000 rows:

```
X_train shape: (50000, 32, 32, 3)
y_train shape: (50000, 1)
X_test shape: (10000, 32, 32, 3)
y_test shape: (10000, 1)
```

In the next recipe, we look at how to load the CIFAR-100 dataset.

CIFAR-100 dataset

A training dataset of 50,000 32 x 32 pixel color images labeled over 100 categories and 10,000 test images, this dataset is similar to CIFAR-10, but it has 100 classes with 600 images in each class. Five-hundred training images and 100 testing images are in each class. The 100 classes in CIFAR-100 are grouped into 20 superclasses. Each image comes with a coarse label (the superclass to which it belongs) and a fine label (the class to which it belongs).

A list of classes in CIFAR-100 is as follows:

Superclass	Classes
aquatic mammals	beaver, dolphin, otter, seal, and whale
fish	aquarium fish, flatfish, ray, shark, and trout
flowers	orchids, poppies, roses, sunflowers, and tulips
food containers	bottles, bowls, cans, cups, and plates
fruit and vegetables	apples, mushrooms, oranges, pears, and sweet peppers
household electrical devices	clock, computer keyboard, lamp, telephone, and television
household furniture	bed, chair, couch, table, and wardrobe
insects	bee, beetle, butterfly, caterpillar, and cockroach
large carnivores	bear, leopard, lion, tiger, and wolf
large man-made outdoor things	bridge, castle, house, road, and skyscraper
large natural outdoor scenes	cloud, forest, mountain, plain, and sea

large omnivores and herbivores	camel, cattle, chimpanzee, elephant, and kangaroo
medium-sized mammals	fox, porcupine, possum, raccoon, and skunk
non-insect invertebrates	crab, lobster, snail, spider, and worm
people	baby, boy, girl, man, and woman
reptiles	crocodile, dinosaur, lizard, snake, and turtle
small mammals	hamster, mouse, rabbit, shrew, and squirrel
trees	maple, oak, palm, pine, and willow
vehicles 1	bicycle, bus, motorcycle, pickup truck, and train
vehicles 2	lawn-mower, rocket, streetcar, tank, and tractor

Reference: `https://www.cs.toronto.edu/~kriz/cifar.html`.

How to do it...

Let's look at how to load this dataset and print the shapes for `X_train`, `y_train`, `X_test`, and `y_test`. The CIFAR-100 dataset is available through the `load_data()` function in `keras.datasets.cifar100`.

The dataset is downloaded from `https://www.cs.toronto.edu/~kriz/cifar-100-python.tar.gz`; this is hidden in the following implementation:

```
from keras.datasets import cifar100
(X_train, y_train), (X_test, y_test) = cifar100.load_data()
print("X_train shape: " + str(X_train.shape))
print("y_train shape: " + str(y_train.shape))
print("X_test shape: " + str(X_test.shape))
print("y_test shape: " + str(y_test.shape))
```

The output of the preceding listing sizes is shown in the following snippet:

```
X_train shape: (50000, 32, 32, 3)
y_train shape: (50000, 1)
X_test shape: (10000, 32, 32, 3)
y_test shape: (10000, 1)
```

Specifying the label mode

This can be specified by a flag in the `load_data()` function:

```
(X_train, y_train), (X_test, y_test) =
cifar100.load_data(label_mode='fine')
```

MNIST dataset

MNIST is a dataset of 60,000 28 x 28 pixel grayscale images of 10 digits. It also contains a test set of 10,000 images. The dataset consists of the following four files:

- `train-images-idx3-ubyte.gz`: Training set images (9912422 bytes), go to `http://yann.lecun.com/exdb/mnist/train-images-idx3-ubyte.gz`
- `train-labels-idx1-ubyte.gz`: Training set labels (28881 bytes), go to `http://yann.lecun.com/exdb/mnist/train-labels-idx1-ubyte.gz`
- `t10k-images-idx3-ubyte.gz`: Test set images (1648877 bytes), go to `http://yann.lecun.com/exdb/mnist/t10k-images-idx3-ubyte.gz`
- `t10k-labels-idx1-ubyte.gz`: Test set labels (4542 bytes), go to `http://yann.lecun.com/exdb/mnist/t10k-labels-idx1-ubyte.gz`

Data in these files is stored in the IDX format. The IDX file format is a format for vectors and multidimensional matrices of various numerical types. You can find more info on the IDX format at `http://www.fon.hum.uva.nl/praat/manual/IDX_file_format.html`:

The preceding image shows the MNIST dataset representation images.

How to do it...

Let's look at the code on how to load MNIST data into numpy arrays using the `keras.datasets.mnist` class:

```
from keras.datasets import mnist
(X_train, y_train), (X_test, y_test) = mnist.load_data()
print("X_train shape: " + str(X_train.shape))
print("y_train shape: " + str(y_train.shape))
print("X_test shape: " + str(X_test.shape))
print("y_test shape: " + str(y_test.shape))
```

The output of the preceding list shows the following dataset shape:

```
X_train shape: (60000, 28, 28)
y_train shape: (60000,)
X_test shape: (10000, 28, 28)
y_test shape: (10000,)
```

Next, let's look at how to load data from a .csv file.

Load data from a CSV file

Keras can take data directly from a numpy array in addition to preexisting datasets.

How to do it...

Let's take an existing .csv file from the internet and use it to create a Keras dataset:

```
dataset =
numpy.loadtxt("https://raw.githubusercontent.com/jbrownlee/Datasets/master/
pima-indians-diabetes.data.csv", delimiter=",")
# split into input (X) and output (Y) variables
X = dataset[:,0:8]
Y = dataset[:,8]
```

Note that the dataset can be directly loaded from the URL with the .csv file.

The output of the preceding code is listed in the following snippet:

```
[ 6. 148. 72. 35. 0. 33.6 0.627 50. ]
1.0
```

Models in Keras – getting started

Let's look at creating a basic model in Keras.

Anatomy of a model

Model is a subclass of Network. The Model class adds training and evaluation routines to a Network. The following diagram shows the relationship between the various classes.

A network is not a class that developers use directly, so some info in this section is for your information only.

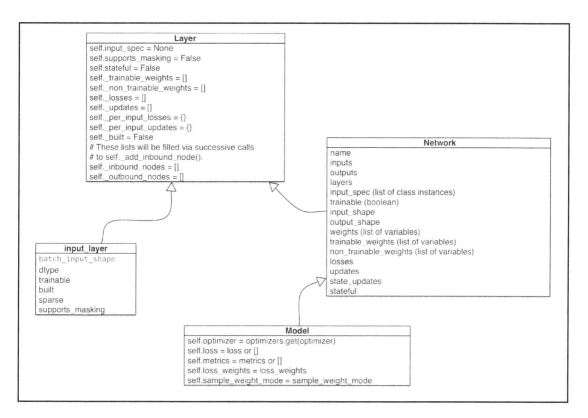

Types of models

There are two types of models in Keras:

- Sequential models
- Models created using functional APIs

Sequential models

A Sequential model can be created by passing a stack of layers to the constructor of a class called **Sequential**.

How to do it...

Creating a basic Sequential mode involves specifying one or more layers.

Create a Sequential model

We will create a Sequential network with four layers.

1. Layer 1 is a dense layer which has `input_shape` of (*, 784) and an `output_shape` of (*, 32)

     A dense layer is a regular densely-connected neural network layer. A Dense layer implements the operation *output = activation(dot(input, kernel) + bias)*, where activation is the element-wise `activation` function passed as the `activation` argument, kernel is a weights matrix created by the layer, and bias is a bias vector created by the layer. (This is only applicable if `use_bias` is `True`).

2. Layer 2 is an activation layer with the `tanh` `Activation` function applies activation to the incoming tensor:

    ```
    keras.layers.Activation(activation)
    ```

    `Activation` can also be applied as a parameter to the dense layer:

    ```
    model.add(Dense(64, activation='tanh'))
    ```

3. Layer 3 is a dense layer with output `(*,10)`

4. Layer 4 has `Activation` that applies the `softmax` function:

    ```
    Activation('softmax')
    ```

In mathematics, the `softmax` function, also called the **normalized exponential function**, is a generalization of the logistic function that squashes a K-dimensional vector z of arbitrary real values to a K-dimensional vector σ(z) of real values; each entry is in the range (0, 1), and all the entries add up to 1. The following formula shows this:

$$\sigma(\mathbf{z})_j = \frac{e^{z_j}}{\sum_{k=1}^{K} e^{z_k}}.$$

```
from keras.models import Sequential
from keras.layers import Dense, Activation
model = Sequential([
  Dense(32, input_shape=(784,)),
  Activation('tanh'),
  Dense(10),
  Activation('softmax'),
])
print(model.summary())
```

5. The summary of the model created is printed in the following snippet:

```
Layer (type) Output Shape Param #
=================================================================
dense_1 (Dense) (None, 32) 25120
_____
activation_1 (Activation) (None, 32) 0
_____
dense_2 (Dense) (None, 10) 330
_____
activation_2 (Activation) (None, 10) 0
=================================================================
Total params: 25,450
Trainable params: 25,450
Non-trainable params: 0
_____
```

`Sequential` is a subclass of `Model` and has some additional methods, as shown in the following sections.

Compile the model

Model is compiled using the method signature:

```
compile(optimizer, loss=None, metrics=None, loss_weights=None,
sample_weight_mode=None, weighted_metrics=None, target_tensors=None)
```

Please refer to the docs for details on what each parameter means: https://keras.io/
models/sequential/#the-sequential-model-api.

Train the model

This method is used to train the model for a given number of epochs (iterations on a dataset):

```
fit(x=None, y=None, batch_size=None, epochs=1, verbose=1, callbacks=None,
validation_split=0.0, validation_data=None, shuffle=True,
class_weight=None, sample_weight=None, initial_epoch=0,
steps_per_epoch=None, validation_steps=None)
```

Please refer to the docs for details on what each parameter means: https://keras.io/
models/sequential/#the-sequential-model-api.

Evaluate the model

The evaluate method is used to evaluate metrics of the model, done using batches:

```
evaluate(x=None, y=None, batch_size=None, verbose=1, sample_weight=None,
steps=None)
```

Predict using the model

Call the following predict API to make the prediction. It returns a numpy array:

```
predict(x, batch_size=None, verbose=0, steps=None)
```

Let's look at an example that uses all these APIs together.

Putting it all together

We will be using the diabetes dataset from Pima Indians.

 This dataset is originally from the *National Institute of Diabetes and Digestive and Kidney Diseases*. The objective of the dataset is to diagnostically predict whether or not a patient has diabetes, based on certain diagnostic measurements included in the dataset. Several constraints were placed on the selection of these instances from a larger database. In particular, all patients here are females, at least 21 years old, and of Pima Indian heritage. The datasets consist of several medical predictor variables and one target variable, outcome. Predictor variables include the number of pregnancies the patient has had, their BMI, insulin level, age, and so on.

```
from keras.models import Sequential
from keras.layers import Dense
import numpy
# fix random seed for reproducibility
numpy.random.seed(7)
# load pima indians dataset
dataset = numpy.loadtxt("data/diabetes.csv", delimiter=",", skiprows=1)
# split into input (X) and output (Y) variables
X = dataset[:,0:8]
Y = dataset[:,8]
# create model
model = Sequential()
model.add(Dense(12, input_dim=8, activation='relu'))
model.add(Dense(8, activation='relu'))
model.add(Dense(1, activation='sigmoid'))
# Compile model
model.compile(loss='binary_crossentropy', optimizer='adam',
metrics=['accuracy'])
# Fit the model
model.fit(X, Y, epochs=150, batch_size=10)
# evaluate the model
scores = model.evaluate(X, Y)
print("\n%s: %.2f%%" % (model.metrics_names[1], scores[1]*100))
```

The dataset shape is `(768, 9)`.

Let's look at the value of the dataset:

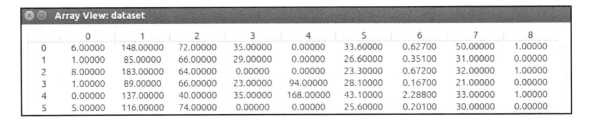

	0	1	2	3	4	5	6	7	8
0	6.00000	148.00000	72.00000	35.00000	0.00000	33.60000	0.62700	50.00000	1.00000
1	1.00000	85.00000	66.00000	29.00000	0.00000	26.60000	0.35100	31.00000	0.00000
2	8.00000	183.00000	64.00000	0.00000	0.00000	23.30000	0.67200	32.00000	1.00000
3	1.00000	89.00000	66.00000	23.00000	94.00000	28.10000	0.16700	21.00000	0.00000
4	0.00000	137.00000	40.00000	35.00000	168.00000	43.10000	2.28800	33.00000	1.00000
5	5.00000	116.00000	74.00000	0.00000	0.00000	25.60000	0.20100	30.00000	0.00000

Values of **X**, which is columns 0 to 7:

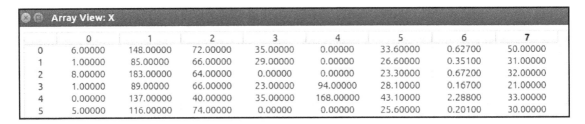

	0	1	2	3	4	5	6	7
0	6.00000	148.00000	72.00000	35.00000	0.00000	33.60000	0.62700	50.00000
1	1.00000	85.00000	66.00000	29.00000	0.00000	26.60000	0.35100	31.00000
2	8.00000	183.00000	64.00000	0.00000	0.00000	23.30000	0.67200	32.00000
3	1.00000	89.00000	66.00000	23.00000	94.00000	28.10000	0.16700	21.00000
4	0.00000	137.00000	40.00000	35.00000	168.00000	43.10000	2.28800	33.00000
5	5.00000	116.00000	74.00000	0.00000	0.00000	25.60000	0.20100	30.00000

The value of **Y** is the 8th column of the dataset, as shown in the following screenshot:

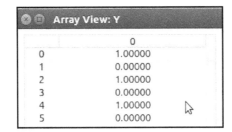

	0
0	1.00000
1	0.00000
2	1.00000
3	0.00000
4	1.00000
5	0.00000

Model inspection internals

On model inspection in the debugger, the following attributes can be found before calling the `compile` method:

```
input=Tensor("dense_1_input:0", shape=(?, 8), dtype=float32)
input_names=<class 'list'>: ['dense_1_input']
input_shape=<class 'tuple'>: (None, 8)
inputs=<class 'list'>: [<tf.Tensor 'dense_1_input:0' shape=(?, 8)
dtype=float32>]
layers=<class 'list'>: [
<keras.layers.core.Dense object at 0x7fdbcbb444a8>,
```

```
<keras.layers.core.Dense object at 0x7fdbcbb05c50>,
<keras.layers.core.Dense object at 0x7fdbcbb05cf8>]
output=Tensor("dense_3/Sigmoid:0", shape=(?, 1), dtype=float32)
output_names=<class 'list'>: ['dense_3']
output_shape=<class 'tuple'>: (None, 1)
outputs-<class 'list'>: [<tf.Tensor 'dense_3/Sigmoid:0' shape=(?, 1)
dtype=float32>]
trainable_weights=<class 'list'>:
 [<tf.Variable 'dense_1/kernel:0' shape=(8, 12) dtype=float32_ref>,
  <tf.Variable 'dense_1/bias:0' shape=(12,) dtype=float32_ref>,
  <tf.Variable 'dense_2/kernel:0' shape=(12, 8) dtype=float32_ref>,
  <tf.Variable 'dense_2/bias:0' shape=(8,) dtype=float32_ref>,
  <tf.Variable 'dense_3/kernel:0' shape=(8, 1) dtype=float32_ref>,
  <tf.Variable 'dense_3/bias:0' shape=(1,) dtype=float32_ref>]
  weights=<class 'list'>:
[<tf.Variable 'dense_1/kernel:0' shape=(8, 12) dtype=float32_ref>,
 <tf.Variable 'dense_1/bias:0' shape=(12,) dtype=float32_ref>,
 <tf.Variable 'dense_2/kernel:0' shape=(12, 8) dtype=float32_ref>,
 <tf.Variable 'dense_2/bias:0' shape=(8,) dtype=float32_ref>,
 <tf.Variable 'dense_3/kernel:0' shape=(8, 1) dtype=float32_ref>,
 <tf.Variable 'dense_3/bias:0' shape=(1,) dtype=float32_ref>]
```

Model compilation internals

Let's look at what happens behind the scenes when `model.compile()` is called.

Get the optimizer depending on the Backend:

Here is a list of the optimizers supported:

```
all_classes = {
'sgd': SGD,
'rmsprop': RMSprop,
'adagrad': Adagrad,
'adadelta': Adadelta,
'adam': Adam,
'adamax': Adamax,
'nadam': Nadam,
'tfoptimizer': TFOptimizer,
}
```

Initialize the loss

The loss is binary `cross_entropy`.

 Cross-entropy loss, also called **log loss**, measures the performance of a model (classification model). The output is a probability value between 0 and 1. Cross-entropy loss increases as the predicted probability diverges from the actual value: $-(y \log(p) + (1 - y) \log(1 - p))$.

```
self.loss = loss or []
```

Initialize all internal variables for output:

```
self._feed_outputs = []
self._feed_output_names = []
self._feed_output_shapes = []
self._feed_loss_fns = []
```

Prepare the targets of the model:

```
self._feed_targets.append(target)
self._feed_outputs.append(self.outputs[i])
self._feed_output_names.append(name)
self._feed_output_shapes.append(shape)
self._feed_loss_fns.append(self.loss_functions[i])
```

Prepare sample weights:

Before compilation, the following values are assigned to sample weights and `sample_weight_modes`:

```
sample_weights = []
sample_weight_modes = []
```

After running through the code execution, it gets initialized to the following values:

```
Tensor("dense_3_sample_weights:0", shape=(?,), dtype=float32)
```

Prepare the metrics:

Next, we prepare metric names and `metrics_tensors`, which store the actual metrics:

```
self.metrics_names = ['loss']
self.metrics_tensors = []
```

Prepare total loss and metrics:

The loss is calculated and appended to `self.metrics_tensors`:

```
output_loss = weighted_loss(y_true, y_pred,
  sample_weight, mask)
...
self.metrics_tensors.append(output_loss)
self.metrics_names.append(self.output_names[i] + '_loss')
```

Next, we calculate nested metrics and `nested_weighted_metrics`:

```
nested_metrics = collect_metrics(metrics, self.output_names)
nested_weighted_metrics = collect_metrics(weighted_metrics,
self.output_names)
```

Initialize the test, train, and predict functions:

These are initialized lazily:

```
self.train_function = None
self.test_function = None
self.predict_function = None
```

Sort trainable weights:

In the end, we initialize the trainable weights:

```
trainable_weights = self.trainable_weights
self._collected_trainable_weights = trainable_weights
```

Model training

In model training, we call `model.fit`, where in the following steps are executed:

Data validation:

When passing `validation_data` to the Keras model, it must contain two parameters (x_val, y_val) or three parameters (x_val, y_val, and `val_sample_weights`).

Output of the sample

The final output of the model metrics from the preceding code is shown in the following code:

```
10/768 [..............................] - ETA: 0s - loss: 0.5371 - acc:
0.7000
400/768 [==============>...............] - ETA: 0s - loss: 0.4888 - acc:
0.7625
768/768 [==============================] - 0s 131us/step - loss: 0.4727 -
acc: 0.7656
Epoch 150/150
10/768 [..............................] - ETA: 0s - loss: 0.3373 - acc:
0.9000
470/768 [================>.............] - ETA: 0s - loss: 0.4534 - acc:
0.7894
768/768 [==============================] - 0s 122us/step - loss: 0.4783 -
acc: 0.7799
32/768 [>.............................] - ETA: 0s
768/768 [==============================] - 0s 51us/step
acc: 77.60%
```

Shared layer models

Multiple layers in Keras can share the output from one layer. There can be multiple different feature extraction layers from an input, or multiple layers can be used to predict the output from a feature extraction layer.

Let's look at both of these examples.

Introduction – shared input layer

In this section, we show how multiple convolutional layers with differently sized kernels interpret an image input. The model takes colored CIFAR images with a size of 32 x 32 x 3 pixels. There are two CNN feature extraction submodels that share this input; the first has a kernel size of 4, the second a kernel size of 8. The outputs from these feature extraction submodels are flattened into vectors and concatenated into one long vector, and this is passed on to a fully connected layer for interpretation before a final output layer makes a binary classification.

This is the model topology:

- One input layer
- Two feature extraction layers
- One interpretation layer
- One dense output layer

How to do it...

First, we need to define the appropriate layers using the Keras APIs. The key API here is creating a merge layer and using it to create an interpretation layer.

Concatenate function

The concatenate function is used to merge two models, as shown in the following code:

```
# merge feature extractors
merge = concatenate([flat1, flat2])
# interpretation layer
hidden1 = Dense(512, activation='relu')(merge)
```

Here is the complete model topology code:

```
#input layer
visible = Input(shape=(32,32,3))
# first feature extractor
conv1 = Conv2D(32, kernel_size=4, activation='relu')(visible)
pool1 = MaxPooling2D(pool_size=(2, 2))(conv1)
flat1 = Flatten()(pool1)
# second feature extractor
conv2 = Conv2D(16, kernel_size=8, activation='relu')(visible)
pool2 = MaxPooling2D(pool_size=(2, 2))(conv2)
flat2 = Flatten()(pool2)
# merge feature extractors
merge = concatenate([flat1, flat2])
# interpretation layer
hidden1 = Dense(512, activation='relu')(merge)
# prediction output
output = Dense(10, activation='sigmoid')(hidden1)
model = Model(inputs=visible, outputs=output)
```

The model topology is saved to a file and shows how a single input layer feeds into two feature extraction layers, as shown in the following diagram:

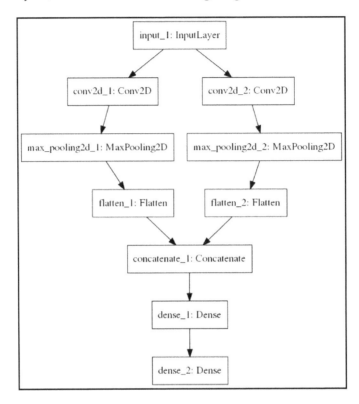

Next, let's compile this model, pass the training dataset, and calculate the accuracy:

```
# Let's train the model using RMSprop
model.compile(loss='categorical_crossentropy',
  optimizer=opt,
  metrics=['accuracy'])
model.fit(x_train, y_train,
  batch_size=batch_size,
  epochs=epochs,
  validation_data=(x_test, y_test),
  shuffle=True)
scores = model.evaluate(x_test, y_test, verbose=1)
print('Test loss:', scores[0])
print('Test accuracy:', scores[1])
```

In the next section, we look at how to use Keras functional APIs to create models and create more complex topologies.

Keras functional APIs

Keras functional APIs provide each layer as a function.

How to do it...

1. To use the functional APIs, you need to import the following classes from the keras package:

```
from keras.layers.core import dense, Activation
```

2. Let's use the preceding imported layers as part of the Sequential model:

```
from keras.models import Sequential
from keras.layers.core import dense, Activation
model = Sequential([
  dense(32, input_dim=784),
  Activation("sigmoid"),
  dense(10),
  Activation("softmax"),
])
model.compile(loss="categorical_crossentropy", optimizer="adam")
```

3. Let's run the previous functional API-based model on MNIST:

```
from keras.utils import plot_model
from keras.layers import Flatten
from keras.models import Sequential
from keras.layers.core import Dense, Activation
from keras.datasets import mnist
import keras

num_classes = 10
batch_size = 32
epochs = 10
batch_size = 128
num_classes = 10
epochs = 12

# input image dimensions
```

```
img_rows, img_cols = 28, 28

# the data, split between train and test sets
(x_train, y_train), (x_test, y_test) = mnist.load_data()

y_train = keras.utils.to_categorical(y_train, num_classes)
y_test = keras.utils.to_categorical(y_test, num_classes)


# input layer
model = Sequential([
  Flatten(input_shape=(28, 28)),
  Dense(32, input_dim=784),
  Activation("sigmoid"),
  Dense(10),
  Activation("softmax"),
])

# summarize layers
print(model.summary())

# plot graph
plot_model(model, to_file='shared_input_layer.png')

opt = keras.optimizers.rmsprop(lr=0.0001, decay=1e-6)

# Let's train the model using RMSprop
model.compile(loss='categorical_crossentropy',
              optimizer=opt,
              metrics=['accuracy'])


model.fit(x_train, y_train,
          batch_size=batch_size,
          epochs=epochs,
          validation_data=(x_test, y_test),
          shuffle=True)

scores = model.evaluate(x_test, y_test, verbose=1)
print('Test loss:', scores[0])
print('Test accuracy:', scores[1])
```

Notice how we flatten the input before feeding it into the model using the first layer:

```
Flatten(input_shape=(28, 28)),
```

The output of the example

The following is the output (though please note this is truncated output):

```
50560/60000 [==========================>.....] - ETA: 0s - loss: 0.3895 -
acc: 0.8933
53504/60000 [==========================>....] - ETA: 0s - loss: 0.3894 -
acc: 0.8929
57216/60000 [===========================>..] - ETA: 0s - loss: 0.3889 -
acc: 0.8928
60000/60000 [=============================] - 1s 17us/step - loss: 0.3886
- acc: 0.8928 - val_loss: 0.3846 - val_acc: 0.8925
32/10000 [..............................] - ETA: 0s
 2592/10000 [======>.......................] - ETA: 0s
 5184/10000 [==============>...............] - ETA: 0s
 8064/10000 [========================>......] - ETA: 0s
10000/10000 [=============================] - 0s 19us/step
Test loss: 0.3846480777263641
Test accuracy: 0.8925
```

Keras functional APIs – linking the layers

In the functional model, we must create and define an input layer, which specifies the shape of the input data. The input layer takes a `shape` argument that is a tuple, which indicates the dimensionality of the input data. When the input data is one-dimensional (for example, for a multilayer perceptron), the shape must leave space for the shape of the mini-batch size, which is determined while splitting the data when training the network. The shape tuple is always defined with an open last dimension when the input is a one-dimensional example (32).

How to do it...

In the following code, we define the first layer:

```
from keras.layers import Input
visible = Input(shape=(32,))
```

We connect the layers together:

```
visible = Input(shape=(32,))
hidden = Dense(32)(visible)
```

Model class

Here we can use the `Model` class to create the model instance, as shown in the following snippet:

```
from keras.models import Model
from keras.layers import Input
from keras.layers import Dense

visible = Input(shape=(32,))
hidden = Dense(32)(visible)
model = Model(inputs=visible, outputs=hidden)
```

We define `Model` with multiple inputs and outputs:

```
model = Model(inputs=[a1, a2], outputs=[b1, b2, b3])
```

In the preceding code, we have multiple layers defined as inputs and outputs. In the next recipe, let's look at how Keras functional APIs can be used for image classification.

Image classification using Keras functional APIs

We have seen how a Sequential model can be used to create an image classification model for MNIST. Let's look at how we can look at convolutional APIs along with the functional APIs. We will explore convolutional APIs from Keras in a later part of the book, so here we focus on the functional aspects of the APIs.

How to do it...

Let's first look at how we will build the model from the input of MNIST images coming in batches:

```
input_shape = (28, 28)
inputs = Input(input_shape)
print(input_shape + (1, ))
# add one more dimension for convolution
x = Reshape(input_shape + (1, ), input_shape=input_shape)(inputs)
conv1 = Conv2D(14, kernel_size=4, activation='relu')(x)
pool1 = MaxPooling2D(pool_size=(2, 2))(conv1)
conv2 = Conv2D(7, kernel_size=4, activation='relu')(pool1)
pool2 = MaxPooling2D(pool_size=(2, 2))(conv2)
```

```
flatten = Flatten()(pool2)
output = Dense(10, activation='sigmoid')(flatten)
model = Model(inputs=inputs, outputs=output)
```

We start with the `input_shape` of `(28, 28)`. This is used to define the input layer:

```
inputs = Input(input_shape)
```

Then we add another dimension to it for convolution and reshape it using the `Reshape` layer:

```
x = Reshape(input_shape + (1, ), input_shape=input_shape)(inputs)
```

Let's define two convolutional layers and pooling layers:

```
conv1 = Conv2D(14, kernel_size=4, activation='relu')(x)
pool1 = MaxPooling2D(pool_size=(2, 2))(conv1)
conv2 = Conv2D(7, kernel_size=4, activation='relu')(pool1)
pool2 = MaxPooling2D(pool_size=(2, 2))(conv2)
```

This is the `model` creation:

```
model = Model(inputs=inputs, outputs=output)
# summarize layers
print(model.summary())
# plot graph
plot_model(model, to_file='convolutional_neural_network.png')
```

The output of the `model` summary is listed in the following code snippet:

```
Using TensorFlow backend.
(28, 28, 1)
_____
Layer (type) Output Shape Param #
=================================================================
input_1 (InputLayer) (None, 28, 28) 0
_____
reshape_1 (Reshape) (None, 28, 28, 1) 0
_____
conv2d_1 (Conv2D) (None, 25, 25, 14) 238
_____
max_pooling2d_1 (MaxPooling2 (None, 12, 12, 14) 0
_____
conv2d_2 (Conv2D) (None, 9, 9, 7) 1575
_____
max_pooling2d_2 (MaxPooling2 (None, 4, 4, 7) 0
_____
flatten_1 (Flatten) (None, 112) 0
```

```
dense_1 (Dense) (None, 10) 1130
=================================================================
Total params: 2,943
Trainable params: 2,943
Non-trainable params: 0
```

Let's also look at the `model` plot:

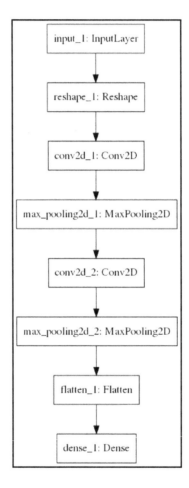

Having looked at how the model is tied together, the following is the complete code listing, which ties everything together:

```
from keras.layers import Flatten
from keras.datasets import mnist
import keras
from keras.utils import plot_model
from keras.models import Model
from keras.layers import Input
from keras.layers import Dense
from keras.layers import Reshape
from keras.layers.convolutional import Conv2D
from keras.layers.pooling import MaxPooling2D

num_classes = 10
batch_size = 32
epochs = 10
batch_size = 128
num_classes = 10
epochs = 12

# input image dimensions
img_rows, img_cols = 28, 28

# the data, split between train and test sets
(x_train, y_train), (x_test, y_test) = mnist.load_data()

y_train = keras.utils.to_categorical(y_train, num_classes)
y_test = keras.utils.to_categorical(y_test, num_classes)

input_shape = (28, 28)
inputs = Input(input_shape)
print(input_shape + (1, ))
# add one more dimension for convolution
x = Reshape(input_shape + (1, ), input_shape=input_shape)(inputs)
conv1 = Conv2D(14, kernel_size=4, activation='relu')(x)
pool1 = MaxPooling2D(pool_size=(2, 2))(conv1)
conv2 = Conv2D(7, kernel_size=4, activation='relu')(pool1)
pool2 = MaxPooling2D(pool_size=(2, 2))(conv2)
flatten = Flatten()(pool2)
output = Dense(10, activation='sigmoid')(flatten)
model = Model(inputs=inputs, outputs=output)
# summarize layers
print(model.summary())
# plot graph
plot_model(model, to_file='convolutional_neural_network.png')

opt = keras.optimizers.rmsprop(lr=0.0001, decay=1e-6)
```

```
# Let's train the model using RMSprop
model.compile(loss='categorical_crossentropy',
              optimizer=opt,
              metrics=['accuracy'])

model.fit(x_train, y_train, batch_size=batch_size, epochs=epochs,
validation_data=(x_test, y_test), shuffle=True)
scores = model.evaluate(x_test, y_test, verbose=1)
print('Test loss:', scores[0])
print('Test accuracy:', scores[1])
```

The following is the output of the preceding listing:

```
8480/10000 [=========================>.....] - ETA: 0s
8672/10000 [==========================>....] - ETA: 0s
8864/10000 [==========================>....] - ETA: 0s
9056/10000 [===========================>...] - ETA: 0s
9280/10000 [===========================>...] - ETA: 0s
9504/10000 [============================>..] - ETA: 0s
9760/10000 [=============================>.] - ETA: 0s
10000/10000 [==============================] - 2s 239us/step
Test loss: 3.944010387802124
Test accuracy: 0.5415
```

As can be seen, the accuracy is low; it will be fine-tuned in `Chapter 5`, *Implementing Convolutional Neural Networks* on CNN.

3
Data Preprocessing, Optimization, and Visualization

In this chapter, we will cover the following recipes:

- Feature standardization of image data
- Sequence padding
- Model visualization
- Optimization
- Common code for samples
- Optimization with stochastic gradient descent
- Optimization with Adam
- Optimization with AdaDelta
- Optimization with RMSProp

 Here is the source code link: `https://github.com/ml-resources/deeplearning-keras/tree/ed1/ch03`.

Feature standardization of image data

In this recipe, we will look at how Keras can be used for feature standardization of image data.

Getting ready

Make sure the Keras installation and Jupyter Notebook installation have been completed.

How to do it...

We will be using the `mnist` dataset. First, let's plot the `mnist` images without standardization:

```
from keras.datasets import mnist
from matplotlib import pyplot

(X_train, y_train), (X_test, y_test) = mnist.load_data()
# create a grid of 3x3 images
for i in range(0, 9):
    ax = pyplot.subplot(330 + 1 + i)
    pyplot.tight_layout()
    ax.tick_params(axis='x', colors='white')
    ax.tick_params(axis='y', colors='white')
 pyplot.imshow(X_train[i], cmap=pyplot.get_cmap('gray'))
# show the plot
pyplot.show()
```

The output plot will be similar to the following screenshot:

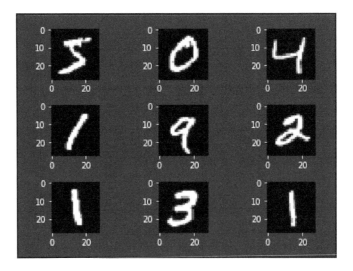

For feature standardization, we are planning to use `ImageDataGenerator`.

Initializing ImageDataGenerator

Use `keras.preprocessing.image.ImageDataGenerator(featurewise_center=False, samplewise_center=False, featurewise_std_normalization=False, samplewise_std_normalization=False)` to initialize `ImageDataGenerator`.

The parameters are explained as follows:

- `featurewise_center`: Boolean. Set input mean to 0 over the dataset, feature-wise.
- `samplewise_center`: Boolean. Set each sample mean to 0.
- `featurewise_std_normalization`: Boolean. Divide inputs by `std` of the dataset, feature-wise.
- `samplewise_std_normalization`: Boolean. Divide each input by its `std`.

Let's apply this to our `mnist` dataset:

```
from keras.preprocessing.image import ImageDataGenerator
from keras import backend as K
K.set_image_dim_ordering('th')

X_train = X_train.reshape(X_train.shape[0], 1, 28, 28)
X_test = X_test.reshape(X_test.shape[0], 1, 28, 28)
# convert from int to float
X_train = X_train.astype('float32')
X_test = X_test.astype('float32')
# define data preparation
datagen = ImageDataGenerator(featurewise_center=True,
featurewise_std_normalization=True,
 samplewise_center=True, samplewise_std_normalization=True)
# fit parameters from data
datagen.fit(X_train)
# configure batch size and retrieve one batch of images
for X_batch, y_batch in datagen.flow(X_train, y_train, batch_size=9):
    # create a grid of 3x3 images
    for i in range(0, 9):
        ax =pyplot.subplot(330 + 1 + i)
        pyplot.tight_layout()
        ax.tick_params(axis='x', colors='white')
        ax.tick_params(axis='y', colors='white')
        pyplot.imshow(X_batch[i].reshape(28, 28),
cmap=pyplot.get_cmap('gray'))
    # show the plot
    pyplot.show()
    break
```

The output of the preceding listing will be a 3 x 3 grid with images standardized and normalized feature-wise, and sample-wise, as shown in the following screenshot:

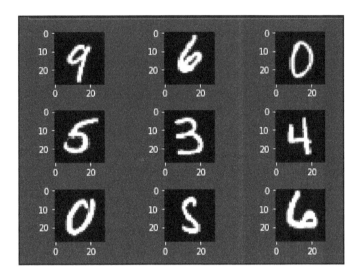

Sequence padding

In this recipe, we will learn how Keras can be used for sequence padding. Padding is useful when sequences are sent in batches to the LSTM network.

Getting ready

Import the function:

```
from keras.preprocessing.sequence import pad_sequences
```

pad_sequences is a function defined as follows:

```
pad_sequences(sequences, maxlen=None, dtype='int32', padding='pre',
truncating='pre', value=0.0)
```

How to do it...

Let's look at the various padding options.

Pre-padding with default 0.0 padding

First, let's look at how to use `pad_sequences` with default pre-padding:

```
from keras.preprocessing.sequence import pad_sequences
# define sequences
sequences = [
[1, 2, 3, 4],
[5, 6, 7],
[5]
]
# pad sequence
padded = pad_sequences(sequences)
print(padded)
```

An output of the preceding `print` statement will show all the sequences padded to length 4.

Post-padding

To pad 0.0 on at the end of shorter arrays, use `padding='post'`, as shown in the following code snippet:

```
padded_post = pad_sequences(sequences,padding='post')
print(padded_post)
```

The preceding output shows how post-padding happens:

Padding with truncation

Let's look at how to use the `maxlen` parameter to truncate `pre` and `post`:

```
padded_maxlen_truncating_pre = pad_sequences(sequences,maxlen=3,
truncating='pre')
print(padded_maxlen_truncating_pre)
```

The output of the preceding code is shown here:

```
[[2 3 4]
 [5 6 7]
 [0 0 5]]
```

In the preceding output, the first value of first row was truncated:

```
padded_maxlen_truncating_post = pad_sequences(sequences,maxlen=3,
truncating='post')
print(padded_maxlen_truncating_post)
```

The output of the preceding code is as follows:

```
[[1 2 3]
 [5 6 7]
 [0 0 5]]
```

In the preceding output, the last value of first row was truncated.

Padding with a non-default value

Let's look at how to pad with a non-default value (1.0, in this case):

```
padded_value = pad_sequences(sequences, value=1.0)
print(padded_value)
```

The following is the output of the preceding code snippet. Notice that all the arrays have been made of length 4 with 1 as the padding value:

```
[[1 2 3 4]
 [1 5 6 7]
 [1 1 1 5]]
```

Model visualization

For simpler models, a simple model summary is sufficient, but for more complex topologies, Keras provides a way to visualize the model. It is a layer on top of the `graphviz` library.

Getting ready

Please make sure `graphviz` is installed:

```
sudo apt-get install graphviz
```

Also, install `pydot`, which is needed in the underlying implementation:

```
sudo pip install pydot
```

How to do it...

Let's take a look at an example where we create a simple model and call `plot_model` on it.

The `plot_model()` function in Keras creates a plot of the neural network. This function takes the following arguments:

- `model`: (required) The model that is to be plotted
- `to_file`: (required) The name of the file to save the plot
- `show_shapes`: (optional, defaults to `False`) Boolean to show the output shapes of each layer
- `show_layer_names`: (optional, defaults to `True`) Boolean to show the name for each layer

The following sections show how `plot_model` can be used.

Code listing

The following code creates a `Sequential` model with two `Dense` layers:

```
from keras.models import Sequential
from keras.layers import Dense
from keras.utils.vis_utils import plot_model
model = Sequential()
model.add(Dense(16, input_dim=1, activation='relu'))
model.add(Dense(16, activation='sigmoid'))
print(model.summary())
```

Keras provides the ability to summarize using the `summary()` method:

```
Using TensorFlow backend.


_____
Layer (type) Output Shape Param #
================================================================
dense_1 (Dense) (None, 16) 32
_____
dense_2 (Dense) (None, 16) 272
================================================================
Total params: 304
Trainable params: 304
Non-trainable params: 0
_____
```

Let's call the `plot_model()` function on this model:

```
plot_model(model, to_file='model_plot.png', show_shapes=True,
show_layer_names=True)
```

The plot is saved in the following file:

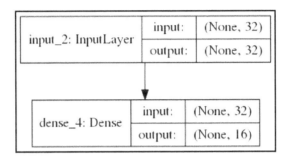

Optimization

Optimization helps in reaching the minima of the loss function between the predicted and actual values of y. Keras supports various optimization techniques, such as the following:

- SGD
- RMS Prop
- Adam
- AdaDelta
- TFOptimizer
- AdaGrad

Common code for samples

The following code list is used by all the samples in optimization. We import the relevant classes:

```
from __future__ import print_function
import keras
from keras.datasets import mnist
from keras.models import Sequential
from keras.layers import Dense, Dropout
```

```
batch_size = 128
num_classes = 10
epochs = 20

(x_train, y_train), (x_test, y_test) = mnist.load_data()

x_train = x_train.reshape(60000, 784)
x_test = x_test.reshape(10000, 784)
x_train = x_train.astype('float32')
x_test = x_test.astype('float32')
x_train /= 255
x_test /= 255
print(x_train.shape[0], 'train samples')
print(x_test.shape[0], 'test samples')
# convert class vectors to binary class matrices

y_train = keras.utils.to_categorical(y_train, num_classes)
y_test = keras.utils.to_categorical(y_test, num_classes)
```

Optimization with stochastic gradient descent

Stochastic gradient descent (**SGD**), in contrast to batch gradient descent, performs a parameter update for each training example, $x^{(i)}$ and label $y^{(i)}$:

$$\Theta = \Theta - \eta \nabla_{\Theta} j(\Theta, x^{(i)}, y^{(i)})$$

Getting ready

Make sure that the preceding common code list is added before the main code snippet in the following codes:

How to do it...

Create a sequential model with the appropriate network topology:

- Input layer with shape *(*, 784)*, and an output of *(*, 512)*
- Hidden layer with an input *(*, 512)* and an output of *(*, 512)*
- Output layer with the input dimension as *(*, 512)* and the output as *(*, 10)*

Let's look at the activation functions for each layer:

- Layer 1 and Layer 1-relu
- Layer 3-softmax

```
from keras.optimizers import SGD

y_train = keras.utils.to_categorical(y_train, num_classes)
y_test = keras.utils.to_categorical(y_test, num_classes)

model = Sequential()
model.add(Dense(512, activation='relu', input_shape=(784,)))
model.add(Dropout(0.2))
model.add(Dense(512, activation='relu'))
model.add(Dropout(0.2))
model.add(Dense(num_classes, activation='softmax'))

model.summary()
sgd = SGD(lr=0.01, decay=1e-6, momentum=0.9, nesterov=True)
model.compile(loss='categorical_crossentropy',
optimizer=SGD(),metrics=['accuracy'])

#model.compile(loss='categorical_crossentropy',
# optimizer=RMSprop(),
# metrics=['accuracy'])

history = model.fit(x_train, y_train,
                    batch_size=batch_size,
                    epochs=epochs,
                    verbose=1,
                    validation_data=(x_test, y_test))
```

Here we are creating a network with two hidden layers and a dropout of 0.2.

Let's look at the optimizer used in RMSProp.

The following is the output of the preceding code:

```
Layer (type) Output Shape Param #
=================================================================
dense_10 (Dense) (None, 512) 401920
_____
dropout_7 (Dropout) (None, 512) 0
_____
dense_11 (Dense) (None, 512) 262656
_____
dropout_8 (Dropout) (None, 512) 0
_____
```

```
dense_12 (Dense) (None, 10) 5130
================================================================
Total params: 669,706
Trainable params: 669,706
Non-trainable params: 0
```

We are want to print the model accuracy and loss as shown in the following snippet:

```
print(history.history.keys())
import matplotlib.pyplot as plt
%matplotlib inline
# summarize history for accuracy
plt.plot(history.history['acc'])
plt.plot(history.history['val_acc'])
plt.title('model accuracy')
plt.ylabel('accuracy')
plt.xlabel('epoch')
plt.legend(['train', 'test'], loc='upper left')
plt.show()
# summarize history for loss
plt.plot(history.history['loss'])
plt.plot(history.history['val_loss'])
plt.title('model loss')
plt.ylabel('loss')
plt.xlabel('epoch')
plt.legend(['train', 'test'], loc='upper left')
plt.show()
```

The graph output for the model accuracy for testing and training data is shown in the following graph. As you can see, both of them converge toward 95%:

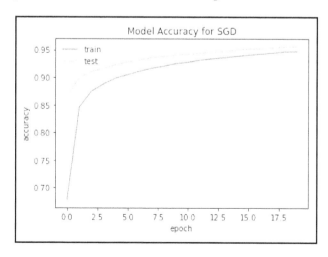

The model loss is shown in the following graph:

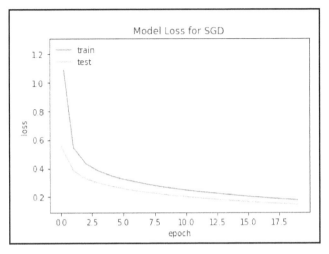

Let's print the final accuracy number:

```
score = model.evaluate(x_test, y_test, verbose=0)
print('Test loss:', score[0])
print('Test accuracy:', score[1])
```

It comes to 0.956, which in itself is quite impressive. Let's look at how to improve it in the following recipes:

```
Test loss: 0.147237592921
Test accuracy: 0.956
```

Optimization with Adam

SGD, in contrast to batch gradient descent, performs a parameter update for *each* training example, $x^{(i)}$ and label $y^{(i)}$:

$$\Theta = \Theta - \eta \nabla_\Theta j(\Theta, x^{(i)}, y^{(i)})$$

Adaptive Moment Estimation (Adam) computes adaptive learning rates for each parameter. Like AdaDelta, Adam not only stores the decaying average of past squared gradients but additionally stores the momentum change for each parameter. Adam works well in practice and is one of the most used optimization methods today.

Adam stores the exponentially decaying average of past gradients (*mt*) in addition to the decaying average of past squared gradients (like Adadelta and RMSprop). Adam behaves like a heavy ball with friction running down the slope leading to a flat minima in the error surface. Decaying averages of past and past squared gradients *mt* and *vt* are computed with the following formulas:

$$m_t = \beta_1 m_{t-1} + (1 - \beta_1) g_t$$

$$v_t = \beta_2 v_{t-1} + (1 - \beta_2) g_t$$

m_t and v_t are estimates of the first moment (the mean) and the second moment (the uncentered variance) of the gradients, respectively, hence the name of the method. As m_t and v_t are initialized as vectors of zeros, the authors of Adam observed that they are biased toward zero, especially during the initial time steps, and especially when the decay rates are small (that is, β_1 and β_2 are close to 1).

The authors counteract these biases by computing bias-corrected first and second-moment estimates. With this, the update rule looks like the following:

$$\hat{m} = \frac{m}{1 - \beta_1^t}$$

$$\hat{v} = \frac{v}{1 - \beta_2^t}$$

$$\Theta_{t+1} = \Theta_t - \frac{\eta}{\sqrt{\hat{v}_t + \epsilon}} \cdot \hat{m}_t$$

Getting ready

Make sure that the preceding common code list is added before the main code snippet in the following code in the next section.

How to do it...

Create a sequential model with the appropriate network topology:

- Input layer with shape (*, 784), and output (*, 512)
- Hidden layer with input (*, 512) and output (*, 512)
- Output layer with input dimension as (*, 512) and output (*, 10)

Activation functions for layer 1 and layer 3 are shown in the points:

- Layer 1 and Layer 1-`relu`
- Layer 3-`softmax`

```
y_train = keras.utils.to_categorical(y_train, num_classes)
y_test = keras.utils.to_categorical(y_test, num_classes)

model = Sequential()
model.add(Dense(512, activation='relu', input_shape=(784,)))
model.add(Dropout(0.2))
model.add(Dense(512, activation='relu'))
model.add(Dropout(0.2))
model.add(Dense(num_classes, activation='softmax'))

model.summary()
adam = keras.optimizers.Adam(lr=0.001, beta_1=0.9, beta_2=0.999,
epsilon=None, decay=0.0, amsgrad=False)
model.compile(loss='categorical_crossentropy',
optimizer=adam,metrics=['accuracy'])


history = model.fit(x_train, y_train,
 batch_size=batch_size,
 epochs=epochs,
 verbose=1,
 validation_data=(x_test, y_test))
```

Here, we are creating a network with two hidden layers and a dropout of 0.2.

The following is the output of the preceding code:

```
Layer (type) Output Shape Param #
=================================================================
dense_10 (Dense) (None, 512) 401920
_____
dropout_7 (Dropout) (None, 512) 0
_____
dense_11 (Dense) (None, 512) 262656
_____
dropout_8 (Dropout) (None, 512) 0
_____
dense_12 (Dense) (None, 10) 5130
=================================================================
Total params: 669,706
Trainable params: 669,706
Non-trainable params: 0
```

Let's print the model accuracy and loss:

```
print(history.history.keys())
import matplotlib.pyplot as plt
%matplotlib inline
# summarize history for accuracy
plt.plot(history.history['acc'])
plt.plot(history.history['val_acc'])
plt.title('model accuracy')
plt.ylabel('accuracy')
plt.xlabel('epoch')
plt.legend(['train', 'test'], loc='upper left')
plt.show()
# summarize history for loss
plt.plot(history.history['loss'])
plt.plot(history.history['val_loss'])
plt.title('model loss')
plt.ylabel('loss')
plt.xlabel('epoch')
plt.legend(['train', 'test'], loc='upper left')
plt.show()
```

The graph output for the model accuracy for testing and training data is shown in the following graph. As you can see, both of them converge toward 95%:

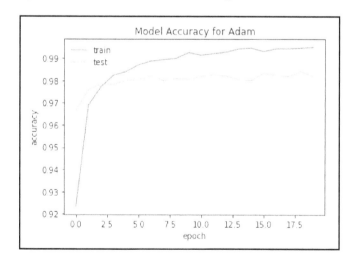

The model loss is shown in the following graph:

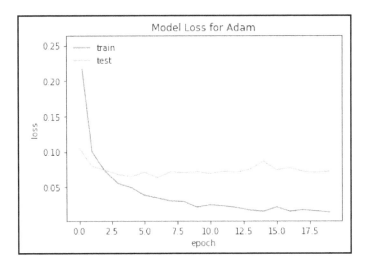

Let's print the final accuracy number:

```
score = model.evaluate(x_test, y_test, verbose=0)
print('Test loss:', score[0])
print('Test accuracy:', score[1])
```

It comes to 0.982, which is much higher than SGD:

```
Test loss: 0.0721200712588
Test accuracy: 0.982
```

In this next recipe, we will look at using RMSProp as another adaptive learning rate method.

Optimization with AdaDelta

AdaDelta solves the problem of the decreasing learning rate in AdaGrad. In AdaGrad, the learning rate is computed as 1 divided by the sum of square roots. At each stage, we add another square root to the sum, which causes the denominator to decrease constantly. Now, instead of summing all prior square roots, it uses a sliding window that allows the sum to decrease.

AdaDelta is an extension of AdaGrad that seeks to reduce its aggressive, monotonically decreasing learning rate. Instead of accumulating all past squared gradients, AdaDelta restricts the window of accumulated past gradients to some fixed size, w.

Instead of inefficiently storing w past squared gradients, the sum of the gradients is recursively defined as a decaying average of all past squared gradients. The running average, $E[g^2]_t$, at time step t then depends (as a fraction, γ, similar to the momentum term) only on the previous average and the current gradient:

$$E\left[g^2\right]_t = \gamma E\left[g^2\right]_{t-1} + \left(1 - \gamma\right)g^2{}_t.$$

Where * $E[g^2]_t$ is the squared sum of gradients for time t * $E[g^2]_{t-1}E[g^2]_{t-1}$ squared sum of gradients for time t-1 * γ, where γ is the fraction of $E[g^2]_{t-1}$ to be added to the rest of the equation.

Assuming a short-term for increment in θ, the following is true:

$$\Delta\theta_t = -\eta \cdot g_{t,i}$$
$$\theta_{t+1} = \theta_t + \Delta\theta_t$$

So the new term for $\Delta\theta$ is as follows:

$$\Delta\theta_t = \frac{-\eta}{\sqrt{E[g^2]_t + \epsilon}}$$

Getting ready

Import the relevant classes, methods, and so on as specified in the preceding common code section.

How to do it...

Create a sequential model with the appropriate topology, as we did in previous sections. In this recipe, the optimizer is the `AdaDelta` implementation in Keras:

```
keras.optimizers.Adadelta(lr=1.0, rho=0.95, epsilon=None, decay=0.0)
```

Adadelta optimizer

It is recommended by the Keras documentation to leave the parameters of this optimizer at their default values.

Let's take a look at the arguments used to initialize this optimizer:

- `lr: float >= 0`: Learning rate. It's recommended to leave it at the default value, `rho: float >= 0`.
- `epsilon: float >= 0`: Fuzz factor. If it is not specified (`None`), it defaults to `K.epsilon()`.
- `decay: float >= 0`: Learning rate decay for each update:

```python
model = Sequential()
model.add(Dense(512, activation='relu', input_shape=(784,)))
model.add(Dropout(0.2))
model.add(Dense(512, activation='relu'))
model.add(Dropout(0.2))
model.add(Dense(num_classes, activation='softmax'))
model.summary()
ada_delta = keras.optimizers.Adadelta(lr=1.0, rho=0.95,
epsilon=None, decay=0.0)
model.compile(loss='categorical_crossentropy',
 optimizer=ada_delta,
 metrics=['accuracy'])

history = model.fit(x_train, y_train,
 batch_size=batch_size,
 epochs=epochs,
 verbose=1,
 validation_data=(x_test, y_test))
```

Here, we are creating a network with two hidden layers and a dropout of `0.2`.

The optimizer we have used is RMSProp for this model.

The following is the output of the preceding code:

```
Layer (type) Output Shape Param #
=================================================================
dense_1 (Dense) (None, 512) 401920
_____
dropout_1 (Dropout) (None, 512) 0
_____
dense_2 (Dense) (None, 512) 262656
_____
```

```
dropout_2 (Dropout) (None, 512) 0
```

```
dense_3 (Dense) (None, 10) 5130
================================================================
Total params: 669,706
Trainable params: 669,706
Non-trainable params: 0
```

Let's plot the model accuracy plot for RMSProp:

```
import matplotlib.pyplot as plt
%matplotlib inline
# summarize history for accuracy
plt.plot(history.history['acc'])
plt.plot(history.history['val_acc'])
plt.title('Model Accuracy for RMSProp')
plt.ylabel('accuracy')
plt.xlabel('epoch')
plt.legend(['train', 'test'], loc='upper left')
plt.show()
# summarize history for loss
plt.plot(history.history['loss'])
plt.plot(history.history['val_loss'])
plt.title('Model Loss for RMSProp')
plt.ylabel('loss')
plt.xlabel('epoch')
plt.legend(['train', 'test'], loc='upper left')
plt.show()
```

The following graph shows the accuracy plot for the AdaDelta-based optimizer:

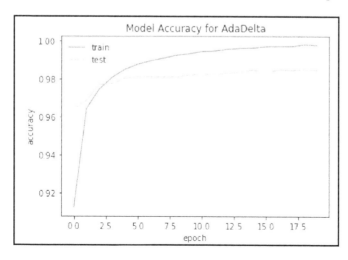

Similarly, the model loss plot for AdaDelta is shown in the following graph:

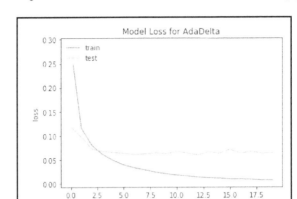

The final test loss and test accuracy with AdaDelta is as follows:

```
score = model.evaluate(x_test, y_test, verbose=0)
print('Test loss:', score[0])
print('Test accuracy:', score[1])
```

The output of the preceding program is shown in the following snippet:

```
Test loss: 0.0644025499775
Test accuracy: 0.9846
```

The accuracy achieved with AdaDelta is higher than plain SGD, Adam, and RMSProp, which was about 0.9846.

Optimization with RMSProp

In this recipe, we look at the code sample on how to optimize with RMSProp.

RMSprop is an (unpublished) adaptive learning rate method proposed by Geoff Hinton. RMSprop and AdaDelta were both developed independently around the same time, stemming from the need to resolve AdaGrad's radically diminishing learning rates. RMSprop is identical to the first update vector of AdaDelta that we derived earlier:

$$E[g^2]_t = 0.9E[g^2]_{t-1} + +0.1g_t^2$$

$$\Theta_{t+1} = \Theta_t - \frac{\eta}{\sqrt{E[g^2]_t + \epsilon}} \cdot g_t$$

RMSprop divides the learning rate by an exponentially decaying average of squared gradients. It is suggested that γ to be set to *0.9*, while a good default value for the learning rate is η is *0.001*.

Getting ready

Import the relevant classes, methods, and so on, as specified in the preceding common code section.

How to do it...

Create a sequential model with the appropriate share:

```
from keras.optimizers import RMSprop
model = Sequential()
model.add(Dense(512, activation='relu', input_shape=(784,)))
model.add(Dropout(0.2))
model.add(Dense(512, activation='relu'))
model.add(Dropout(0.2))
model.add(Dense(num_classes, activation='softmax'))
model.summary()
model.compile(loss='categorical_crossentropy',
 optimizer=RMSprop(),
 metrics=['accuracy'])
history = model.fit(x_train, y_train,
 batch_size=batch_size,
 epochs=epochs,
 verbose=1,
 validation_data=(x_test, y_test))
```

Here we are creating a network with two hidden layers and a dropout of `0.2`.

Optimizer used in RMSProp.

The following is the output of the preceding code:

```
Layer (type) Output Shape Param #
=================================================================
dense_1 (Dense) (None, 512) 401920
_____
dropout_1 (Dropout) (None, 512) 0
_____
dense_2 (Dense) (None, 512) 262656
_____
```

```
dropout_2 (Dropout) (None, 512) 0
```

```
dense_3 (Dense) (None, 10) 5130
============================================================
Total params: 669,706
Trainable params: 669,706
Non-trainable params: 0
```

Let's plot the model accuracy for RMSProp:

```
import matplotlib.pyplot as plt
%matplotlib inline
# summarize history for accuracy
plt.plot(history.history['acc'])
plt.plot(history.history['val_acc'])
plt.title('Model Accuracy for RMSProp')
plt.ylabel('accuracy')
plt.xlabel('epoch')
plt.legend(['train', 'test'], loc='upper left')
plt.show()
# summarize history for loss
plt.plot(history.history['loss'])
plt.plot(history.history['val_loss'])
plt.title('Model Loss for RMSProp')
plt.ylabel('loss')
plt.xlabel('epoch')
plt.legend(['train', 'test'], loc='upper left')
plt.show()
```

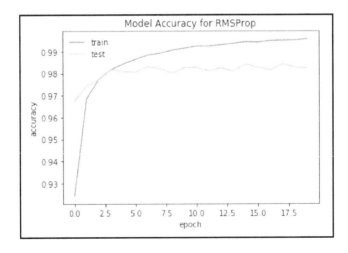

Similarly, the model loss graph is shown in the following graph:

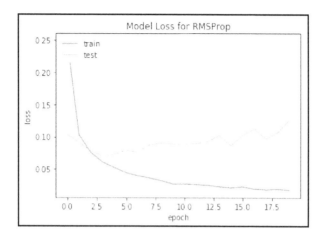

The final test loss and test accuracy with RMSProp is as follows:

```
score = model.evaluate(x_test, y_test, verbose=0)
print('Test loss:', score[0])
print('Test accuracy:', score[1])
```

The output is as follows:

```
Test loss: 0.126795965524
Test accuracy: 0.9824
```

The accuracy achieved with RMSProp is higher than plain SGD, which was about 0.95. It is quite close to the accuracy but lower than that provided by Adam and AdaDelta.

4
Classification Using Different Keras Layers

In this chapter, we will cover the following recipes:

- Classification for breast cancer
- Classification for spam detection

Introduction

Classification is an essential classical problem. The purpose of classification is to automatically classify a text corpus and images into one or more specified classes. In this chapter, we'll use the Keras library to train a classifier. Classification is a general task where machine learning is used, be it question answering, a support request, business question, cancer classification, and so on. This chapter describes how classification problems can be tackled with the open source neural network library. Compared to traditional algorithms, deep learning has several advantages for classification, including flexible models, lower amount of domain expertise being required, and easier ongoing learning.

Classification for breast cancer

We will work on a problem of classification to predict whether a cancer is benign or malignant. We will drive through developing an algorithm that uses neural networks to accurately predict (~94 percent accuracy) if a breast cancer tumor is benign or malignant, basically teaching a machine to predict breast cancer. This may seem difficult, but using Keras APIs, we will have this seemingly complex model ready for use. The dataset description is provided in the following content:

Breast Cancer Wisconsin (Diagnostic) dataset:

Features are computed from a digitized image of a **fine needle aspirate** (**FNA**) of a breast mass. They describe characteristics of the cell nuclei present in the image. A few of the images can be found at `http://www.cs.wisc.edu/~street/images/`.

Class distribution: 357 benign, 212 malignant.

This database is also available via the UW CS FTP server: `ftp ftp.cs.wisc.edu cd math-prog/cpo-dataset/machine-learn/WDBC/`

How to do it...

In this recipe, we will develop a modeling pipeline for classification which tries to classify cancer type. The modeling pipelines use the Adam model written using the Keras functional API. The pipelines also use various data manipulation libraries. We will be using Keras; more specifically, we will be using `sklearn`, `numpy`, and `pandas` to create our model.

Import the following libraries for use. pandas is a data analysis library in Python. The `sklearn` is a machine learning library that is famous for data mining and analysis. Keras is a neural network API that will help us create the actual neural network:

```
import pandas as pd
from sklearn.preprocessing import LabelEncoder, StandardScaler
from sklearn.model_selection import train_test_split
from sklearn.model_selection import GridSearchCV
from keras.wrappers.scikit_learn import KerasClassifier
from keras.models import Sequential, load_model
from keras.layers import Dense
from sklearn.metrics import confusion_matrix
```

Data processing

It is crucial that we serve the right data as input to the neural network architecture for training and validation. We need to make sure that data has useful scale and format and even that meaningful features are included. This will lead to more consistent and better results.

Perform the following steps for data preprocessing:

1. Load the dataset using pandas
2. Split the dataset into the input and output variables for machine learning
3. Apply a preprocessing transform to the input variables
4. Summarize the data to show the change

We use the panda's library to load data and review the shape of our dataset:

```
dataset = pd.read_csv('/deeplearning/google/kaggle/breast-cancer/data.csv')

# get dataset details
print(dataset.head(5))
print(dataset.columns.values)
print(dataset.info())
print(dataset.describe())
```

The output is shown in the following code:

```
id diagnosis       ...       fractal_dimension_worst  Unnamed: 32
0    842302      M   ...                        0.11890         NaN
1    842517      M   ...                        0.08902
NaN
2  84300903      M   ...                        0.08758         NaN
3  84348301      M   ...                        0.17300         NaN
4  84358402      M   ...                        0.07678         NaN
Data columns (total 33 columns):
id                       569 non-null int64
diagnosis                569 non-null object
radius_mean              569 non-null float64
texture_mean             569 non-null float64
perimeter_mean           569 non-null float64
area_mean                569 non-null float64
smoothness_mean          569 non-null float64
compactness_mean         569 non-null float64
concavity_mean           569 non-null float64
concave points_mean      569 non-null float64
symmetry_mean            569 non-null float64
fractal_dimension_mean   569 non-null float64
radius_se                569 non-null float64
```

```
texture_se                    569 non-null float64
perimeter_se                  569 non-null float64
area_se                       569 non-null float64
smoothness_se                 569 non-null float64
compactness_se                569 non-null float64
concavity_se                  569 non-null float64
concave points_se             569 non-null float64
symmetry_se                   569 non-null float64
fractal_dimension_se          569 non-null float64
radius_worst                  569 non-null float64
texture_worst                 569 non-null float64
perimeter_worst               569 non-null float64
area_worst                    569 non-null float64
smoothness_worst              569 non-null float64
compactness_worst             569 non-null float64
concavity_worst               569 non-null float64
concave points_worst          569 non-null float64
symmetry_worst                569 non-null float64
fractal_dimension_worst       569 non-null float64
Unnamed: 32                     0 non-null float64
dtypes: float64(31), int64(1), object(1)
memory usage: 146.8+ KB
None
id         ...        Unnamed: 32
count   5.690000e+02      ...              0.0
mean    3.037183e+07      ...              NaN
std     1.250206e+08      ...              NaN
min     8.670000e+03      ...              NaN
25%     8.692180e+05      ...              NaN
50%     9.060240e+05      ...              NaN
75%     8.813129e+06      ...              NaN
max     9.113205e+08      ...              NaN
```

The output describes the starting values, features, missing values, and distribution of numerical features of the dataset.

In order to teach our machine how to predict whether a tumor is malignant or benign, we need to input it a dataset of previously classified tumors. We have 33 columns where the last column, `Unnamed: 32`, contains all null values, which will be excluded. Our label or the class is called **diagnosis**. We will also not include `id` in our training set, since it does not have any effect on the classification. Thus, we are left with 30 features that are all of type `float64` and do not contain missing values. We will separate the features and labels:

```
# data cleansing
X = dataset.iloc[:, 2:32]
print(X.info())
print(type(X))
```

```
y = dataset.iloc[:, 1]
print(y)
```

The output is shown in the following code:

```
Data columns (total 30 columns):
radius_mean                    569 non-null float64
texture_mean                   569 non-null float64
...
concave points_worst           569 non-null float64
symmetry_worst                 569 non-null float64
fractal_dimension_worst        569 non-null float64
dtypes: float64(30)
memory usage: 133.4 KB
None
<class 'pandas.core.frame.DataFrame'>
0       M
1       M
2       M
3       M
4       M
```

Mark that `diagnosis` contains M or B to represent a malignant or benign tumor. We will encode them to 0 and 1 using `LabelEncoder()`:

```
'''encode the labels to 0, 1 respectively'''
print(y[100:110])
encoder = LabelEncoder()
y = encoder.fit_transform(y)
print([y[100:110]])
```

The output is shown in the following code:

```
Name: diagnosis, dtype: object
[array([1, 0, 0, 0, 0, 1, 0, 0, 1, 0])]
```

We now split data into training and validation sets. The training dataset is used to fit the model and the validation dataset is used to provide an unbiased evaluation of a model fit on the training dataset while tuning model hyperparameters; 80 percent of the data is for training and the other 20% for validation:

```
# lets split dataset now
XTrain, XTest, yTrain, yTest = train_test_split(X, y, test_size=0.2,
random_state=0)
```

Now let's apply feature scaling. Scaling makes sure that simply because certain features are large, the model won't lead to using them as the main predictor:

```
# feature scaling
scalar = StandardScaler()
XTrain = scalar.fit_transform(XTrain)
XTest = scalar.transform(XTest)
```

Modeling

Let's now create a model and add layers to it.. We can work around and modify the number of units, but if we are not sure what number to initialize with then simply initialize the units of all layers except the last one with the (*number of features + number of output nodes/2*), which equals 15 in our case. As explained in the following points, we have to provide an input dimension for the first layer only. `relu` activation refers to the rectified linear unit and `sigmoid` refers to the `sigmoid` activation function. With the help of the `sigmoid` activation function, we can get the probabilities of the classification, which might be beneficial in some cases to conduct further study.

For every model, there are hyperparameters that are set before the learning process starts. Let's first find the hyperparameters using which the model can give more precise predictions. We will tune `batch_size`, `epochs`, and `optimizer`. This will take some time to run.

Tuning is a final step in the pipeline of machine learning before showing results. It is called **hyperparameter optimization**, where the algorithm parameters are referred to as hyperparameters, whereas the coefficients are referred to as **parameters**. Optimization implies the searching nature of the problem. The grid search is a method for parameter tuning that will build and evaluate a model for the various combination of algorithm parameters specified in a grid:

1. `GridSearchCV` provides an exhaustive search over specified parameter values for an estimator:

```
# choosing hyper parameters
def classifier(optimizer):
    model = Sequential()
    model.add(Dense(units=16, kernel_initializer='uniform',
activation='relu', input_dim=30))
    model.add(Dense(units=8, kernel_initializer='uniform',
activation='relu'))
    model.add(Dense(units=6, kernel_initializer='uniform',
activation='relu'))
    model.add(Dense(units=1, kernel_initializer='uniform',
```

```
activation='sigmoid'))
    model.compile(optimizer=optimizer, loss='binary_crossentropy',
metrics=['accuracy'])
    return model


model = KerasClassifier(build_fn=classifier)
params = {'batch_size': [1, 5], 'epochs': [100, 120], 'optimizer':
['adam', 'rmsprop']}
gridSearch = GridSearchCV(estimator=model, param_grid=params,
scoring='accuracy', cv=10)
gridSearch = gridSearch.fit(XTrain, yTrain)
score = gridSearch.best_score_
bestParams = gridSearch.best_params_
print(score)
print(bestParams)
```

The output is shown in the following code:

```
1/455 [..............................] - ETA: 3:36 - loss: 0.6932 -
acc: 0.0000e+00
44/455 [=>............................] - ETA: 4s - loss: 0.6928 -
acc: 0.5227
88/455 [====>.........................] - ETA: 2s - loss: 0.6912 -
acc: 0.6136
130/455 [=======>......................] - ETA: 1s - loss: 0.6849 -
acc: 0.7154
166/455 [=========>....................] - ETA: 1s - loss: 0.6723 -
acc: 0.7530
200/455 [============>.................] - ETA: 0s - loss: 0.6613 -
acc: 0.7850

best_parameters: {'batch_size': 1, 'epochs': 100, 'optimizer':
'rmsprop'}
best_accuracy: 0.998021978022
```

2. Now let's build the neural network with the parameters that we found earlier:

```
# modeling
model = Sequential()
model.add(Dense(units=16, kernel_initializer='uniform',
activation='relu', input_dim=30))
model.add(Dense(units=8, kernel_initializer='uniform',
activation='relu'))
model.add(Dense(units=6, kernel_initializer='uniform',
activation='relu'))
model.add(Dense(units=1, kernel_initializer='uniform',
activation='sigmoid'))
```

3. Compile the classifier using the `adam` optimizer and using `binary_crossentropy` as a loss function, since classification is binary; that is, there are only two classes, M or B:

```
model.compile(optimizer='adam', loss='binary_crossentropy',
metrics=['accuracy'])
```

4. Now let's fit the data. We will train it with a batch size of 1 and 120 epochs and save the model for future classifications:

```
model.fit(XTrain, yTrain, batch_size=1, epochs=120)
model.save('./cancer_model.h5')
```

5. We will not use the model to classify and test the dataset, calculating the training accuracy and confusion matrix:

```
yPred = model.predict(XTest)
yPred = [1 if y > 0.5 else 0 for y in yPred]
matrix = confusion_matrix(yTest, yPred)
print(matrix)
accuracy = (matrix[0][0] + matrix[1][1]) / (matrix[0][0] +
matrix[0][1] + matrix[1][0] + matrix[1][1])
print("Accuracy: " + str(accuracy * 100) + "%")
```

The output is shown in the following code:

```
[[64 3]
 [ 3 44]]
Accuracy: 94.73684210526315%
```

Full code listing

Following is the full code listing of the recipe *Classification for breast cancer*:

```
import pandas as pd
from sklearn.preprocessing import LabelEncoder, StandardScaler
from sklearn.model_selection import train_test_split
from sklearn.model_selection import GridSearchCV
from keras.wrappers.scikit_learn import KerasClassifier
from keras.models import Sequential, load_model
from keras.layers import Dense
from sklearn.metrics import confusion_matrix

dataset = pd.read_csv('/deeplearning/google/kaggle/breast-cancer/data.csv')

# get dataset details
```

```
print(dataset.head(5))
print(dataset.columns.values)
print(dataset.info())
print(dataset.describe())

# data cleansing
X = dataset.iloc[:, 2:32]
print(X.info())
print(type(X))
y = dataset.iloc[:, 1]
print(y)

'''encode the labels to 0, 1 respectively'''
print(y[100:110])
encoder = LabelEncoder()
y = encoder.fit_transform(y)
print([y[100:110]])

# lets split dataset now
XTrain, XTest, yTrain, yTest = train_test_split(X, y, test_size=0.2,
random_state=0)

# feature scaling
scalar = StandardScaler()
XTrain = scalar.fit_transform(XTrain)
XTest = scalar.transform(XTest)

# choosing hyper parameters
'''
def classifier(optimizer):
    model = Sequential()
    model.add(Dense(units=16, kernel_initializer='uniform',
activation='relu', input_dim=30))
    model.add(Dense(units=8, kernel_initializer='uniform',
activation='relu'))
    model.add(Dense(units=6, kernel_initializer='uniform',
activation='relu'))
    model.add(Dense(units=1, kernel_initializer='uniform',
activation='sigmoid'))
    model.compile(optimizer=optimizer, loss='binary_crossentropy',
metrics=['accuracy'])
    return model


model = KerasClassifier(build_fn=classifier)
params = {'batch_size': [1, 5], 'epochs': [100, 120], 'optimizer': ['adam',
'rmsprop']}
gridSearch = GridSearchCV(estimator=model, param_grid=params,
```

```
scoring='accuracy', cv=10)
gridSearch = gridSearch.fit(XTrain, yTrain)
score = gridSearch.best_score_
bestParams = gridSearch.best_params_
print(score)
print(bestParams)
'''

# modeling
model = Sequential()
model.add(Dense(units=16, kernel_initializer='uniform', activation='relu',
input_dim=30))
model.add(Dense(units=8, kernel_initializer='uniform', activation='relu'))
model.add(Dense(units=6, kernel_initializer='uniform', activation='relu'))
model.add(Dense(units=1, kernel_initializer='uniform',
activation='sigmoid'))
model.compile(optimizer='adam', loss='binary_crossentropy',
metrics=['accuracy'])
model.fit(XTrain, yTrain, batch_size=1, epochs=120)
model.save('/Users/manpreet.singh/git/deeplearning/google/kaggle/breast-
cancer/cancer_model.h5')
yPred = model.predict(XTest)
yPred = [1 if y > 0.5 else 0 for y in yPred]
matrix = confusion_matrix(yTest, yPred)
print(matrix)
accuracy = (matrix[0][0] + matrix[1][1]) / (matrix[0][0] + matrix[0][1] +
matrix[1][0] + matrix[1][1])
print("Accuracy: " + str(accuracy * 100) + "%")
```

Classification for spam detection

Spam detection is a common classification problem. In the following recipe, we have the corpus of raw text or documents, including labels of those documents marked spam or no spam. The data source here is the SMS Spam Collection v.1, which is a public set of SMS labeled messages that have been collected for mobile phone spam research.

The dataset can be downloaded from `http://www.dt.fee.unicamp.br/` `~tiago/smsspamcollection/`. The following table lists the provided dataset in different file formats, the number of samples in each class, and the total number of samples:

Application	File format	# Spam	# Ham	Total	Link
General	Plain text	747	4,827	5,574	http://www.dt.fee.unicamp.br/~tiago/ smsspamcollection/smsspamcollection.zip
Weka	ARFF	747	4,827	5,574	http://www.dt.fee.unicamp.br/~tiago/ smsspamcollection/smsSpamCollection.arff

How to do it...

In this recipe, we develop a modeling pipeline for classification that tries to classify the spam type into ham or spam. The modeling pipelines use the RMSProp model written using the Keras functional API.

Import the following libraries for use. pandas is a data analysis library in Python. Numpy is a numerical computation and Keras is a neural network API that will help us create the actual neural network:

```
from keras.layers import SimpleRNN, Embedding, Dense, LSTM
from keras.models import Sequential
from keras.preprocessing.text import Tokenizer
from keras.preprocessing.sequence import pad_sequences
import numpy as np
from sklearn.metrics import confusion_matrix
import matplotlib.pyplot as plt
import pandas as pd
```

Data processing

We will use the panda's library to load data and review the shape of our dataset.

Perform the following steps for data preprocessing:

1. Load the dataset using pandas
2. Convert the labels to `[0,1]`
3. Split the dataset into the input and output variables for machine learning

4. Tokenize the data

5. Summarize the data to show the change:

```
# get dataset
data = pd.read_csv('./data.csv')
texts = []
classes = []
for i, label in enumerate(data['Class']):
    texts.append(data['Text'][i])
    if label == 'ham':
        classes.append(0)
    else:
        classes.append(1)

texts = np.asarray(texts)
classes = np.asarray(classes)

print("number of texts :", len(texts))
print("number of labels: ", len(classes))
```

The output is shown in the following code:

```
number of texts: 5572
number of labels: 5572
```

6. Let's now define the max features and max document length to be used by the classifier:

```
# number of words used as features
maxFeatures = 10000
# max document length
maxLen = 500
```

7. We now split the data into training and validation sets. The training dataset is used to fit the model and the validation dataset is used to provide an unbiased evaluation of a model fit on the training dataset, while tuning model hyperparameters; 80% of the data is for training and the other 20% for validation:

```
# we will use 80% of data as training and 20% as validation data
trainingData = int(len(texts) * .8)
validationData = int(len(texts) - trainingData)
```

8. Words are known as **tokens**, and the method of breaking the text into tokens is described as **tokenization**. The Keras library gives the `Tokenizer()` class for preparing text documents for neural networks. The `tokenizer` should be created and then fit on either raw text documents or integer encoded text documents:

```
# tokenizer
tokenizer = Tokenizer()
tokenizer.fit_on_texts(texts)
sequences = tokenizer.texts_to_sequences(texts)
word_index = tokenizer.word_index
print("Found {0} unique words: ".format(len(word_index)))
data = pad_sequences(sequences, maxlen=maxLen)
print("data shape: ", data.shape)
```

The output is shown in the following code:

```
Found 9006 unique words:
data shape: (5572, 500)
```

9. Finally, we shuffle the dataset and create training and test sets for modeling, described in the next section:

```
# shuffle data
indices = np.arange(data.shape[0])
np.random.shuffle(indices)
data = data[indices]
labels = classes[indices]

X_train = data[:trainingData]
y_train = labels[:trainingData]
X_test = data[trainingData:]
y_test = labels[trainingData:]
```

Modeling

Now, we will create a sequential model using the Keras library, which is internally represented as a sequence of layers. First, we create a new sequential model and add layers to develop the network topology. After the model is defined, we compile it with the backend as TensorFlow. The backend here chooses the best way to represent the network for training and making predictions to run on the given hardware.

We define the embedding layer as part of the network modeling, as shown in the next code snippet. The embedding has the size of a max feature of 32. The model, in this case, is a binary classifier. Finally, we can fit and evaluate the classification model.

We must specify the `loss` function to evaluate a set of weights, the optimizer used to search through different weights for the network, and any optional metrics we would like to collect and report during training. The code is as follows:

```
# modeling
model = Sequential()
model.add(Embedding(maxFeatures, 32))
model.add(LSTM(32))
model.add(Dense(1, activation='sigmoid'))
model.compile(optimizer='rmsprop', loss='binary_crossentropy',
metrics=['acc'])
rnn = model.fit(X_train, y_train, epochs=10, batch_size=60,
validation_split=0.2)
```

The output is shown in the following code:

```
Epoch 1/10
60/3565 [..............................] - ETA: 2:00 - loss: 0.6927 - acc:
0.5833
  120/3565 [>.............................] - ETA: 1:25 - loss: 0.6864 -
acc: 0.7083
  180/3565 [>.............................] - ETA: 1:13 - loss: 0.6812 -
acc: 0.7556
...
Epoch 10/10
3000/3565 [========================>.....] - ETA: 9s - loss: 0.0175 - acc:
0.9933
  3540/3565 [============================>.] - ETA: 0s - loss: 0.0155 - acc:
0.9944
  3565/3565 [==============================] - 61s 17ms/step - loss: 0.0154
- acc: 0.9944 - val_loss: 0.0463 - val_acc: 0.9865
```

Finally, we can evaluate our model on the test data:

```
# predictions
pred = model.predict_classes(X_test)
acc = model.evaluate(X_test, y_test)
proba_rnn = model.predict_proba(X_test)
print("Test loss is {0:.2f} accuracy is {1:.2f}
".format(acc[0],acc[1]))
print(confusion_matrix(pred, y_test))
```

The output is shown in the following code:

```
Test loss is 0.07 accuracy is 0.98
 [[956 15]
 [ 5 139]]
```

Training and validation loss is shown in the following diagram:

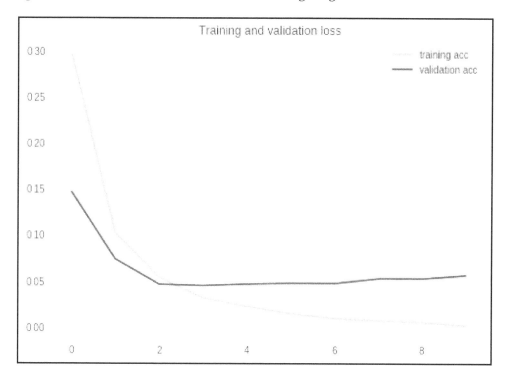

Full code listing

Following is the full code listing of the recipe *Classification for spam detection*:

```
from keras.layers import Embedding, Dense, LSTM
from keras.models import Sequential
from keras.preprocessing.text import Tokenizer
from keras.preprocessing.sequence import pad_sequences
import numpy as np
from sklearn.metrics import confusion_matrix
import pandas as pd

# get dataset
```

```
data = pd.read_csv('/spam-detection/spam_dataset.csv')
texts = []
classes = []
for i, label in enumerate(data['Class']):
    texts.append(data['Text'][i])
    if label == 'ham':
        classes.append(0)
    else:
        classes.append(1)

texts = np.asarray(texts)
classes = np.asarray(classes)

print("number of texts :", len(texts))
print("number of labels: ", len(classes))

# number of words used as features
maxFeatures = 10000
# max document length
maxLen = 500

# we will use 80% data set for training and 20% data set for validation
trainingData = int(len(texts) * .8)
validationData = int(len(texts) - trainingData)

# tokenizer
tokenizer = Tokenizer()
tokenizer.fit_on_texts(texts)
sequences = tokenizer.texts_to_sequences(texts)
word_index = tokenizer.word_index
print("Found {0} unique words: ".format(len(word_index)))
data = pad_sequences(sequences, maxlen=maxLen)
print("data shape: ", data.shape)

indices = np.arange(data.shape[0])
np.random.shuffle(indices)
data = data[indices]
labels = classes[indices]

X_train = data[:trainingData]
y_train = labels[:trainingData]
X_test = data[trainingData:]
y_test = labels[trainingData:]

# modeling
model = Sequential()
model.add(Embedding(maxFeatures, 32))
model.add(LSTM(32))
```

```
model.add(Dense(1, activation='sigmoid'))
model.compile(optimizer='rmsprop', loss='binary_crossentropy',
metrics=['acc'])
rnn = model.fit(X_train, y_train, epochs=10, batch_size=60,
validation_split=0.2)

# predictions
pred = model.predict_classes(X_test)
acc = model.evaluate(X_test, y_test)
proba_rnn = model.predict_proba(X_test)
print("Test loss is {0:.2f} accuracy is {1:.2f}  ".format(acc[0],acc[1]))
print(confusion_matrix(pred, y_test))
```

Implementing Convolutional Neural Networks

5

In this chapter, we will cover the following recipes:

- Cervical cancer classification
- Digit recognition

Introduction

Convolutional neural networks (**CNNs**) are networks of neurons that have learnable weights and biases. Every neuron accepts inputs, calculates a dot product, and follows it with a nonlinearity. CNNs are composed of several convolutional layers and are then followed by one or more fully connected layers, as in a standard multilayer neural network, starting from the raw image pixels on one end to class scores at the other. CNNs preserve the spatial relationship between pixels by learning feature representations. The feature is learned and applied across the whole image, allowing for the objects in the images to be shifted or translated in the scene and still be detectable by the network.

In a nutshell, CNNs are, fundamentally, several layers of convolutions with nonlinear activation functions, such as ReLU or tanh, applied to the results.

Applications for CNNs include relation extraction and relation classification tasks, image moderation, and natural language processing. This list of possibilities for which one can use a CNN are even greater. This chapter's recipes aim to introduce you to CNNs as applied to deep learning models so that you can adapt them to your dataset with ease and develop useful applications.

Cervical cancer classification

Cervical cancer is cancer that occurs in the cervix. Cervical cancer is easy to counter if caught in its early stages. However, due to lack of expertise in the field, one of the biggest challenges for cervical cancer screening and treatment programs is determining a suitable method of treatment. The treatment workflow would be greatly improved given the ability to make real-time determinations about a patients treatment eligibility based on cervix type.

Getting ready

In this recipe, we develop a modeling pipeline that tries to identify a woman's cervix type based on images with greater accuracy. The modeling pipeline uses a CNN models written using the Keras functional API for image classification. The pipeline also use a various image manipulation libraries.

The data for this recipe can be found at `https://www.kaggle.com/c/intel-mobileodt-cervical-cancer-screening`. The dataset is part of the challenge to develop an algorithm that accurately identifies a woman's cervix type based on images. Doing so will prevent ineffectual treatments and allow healthcare providers to give a proper referral for cases that require more advanced treatment.

As a first step, clone the GitHub repository at `https://github.com/ml-resources/deeplearning-keras/tree/ed1/ch05`. Download and save the training and test sets to the `data` folder in the repository:

- `train.7z`: The training set. The images are organized in their labeled categories: `Type_1`, `Type_2`, and `Type_3`.
- `test.7z`: The test set.

To understand more about the background of how these cervix types are defined, please refer to this document: `https://kaggle2.blob.core.windows.net/competitions/kaggle/6243/media/Cervix%20types%20clasification.pdf`).

How to do it...

The training images are assumed to be stored in the `train` folder in subfolders `Type_1`, `Type_2`, and `Type_3`. The images are stored as `.jpg` files in separate folders depending on their classification. Image paths are read as strings; the function uses the image's folder name to get the corresponding label and returns the image paths and labels as two parallel arrays. Let's get started with the data preprocessing steps.

Data processing

Cervical images are of varying sizes and have a high resolution. For CNNs, the incoming data needs to be of uniform size and also needs to have enough resolution to be able to differentiate the main features in classification, but a low enough resolution to avoid computational limits:

```
# process cervical dataset
def processCervicalData():
    # image resizing
    imgPaths = []
    labels = []
    trainingDirs = ['/deeplearning-keras/ch05/data/train']
    for dir in trainingDirs:
        newFilePaths, newLabels, numLabels = readFilePaths(dir)
        if len(newFilePaths) > 0:
            imgPaths += newFilePaths
            labels += newLabels

    imgPaths, labels = shuffle(imgPaths, labels)
    labelCount = labelsCount(labels)

    type1Count = labelCount[0]
    type2Count = labelCount[1]
    type3Count = labelCount[2]

    print("Count of type1 : ", type1Count)
    print("Count of type2 : ", type2Count)
    print("Count of type3 : ", type3Count)
    print("Total Number of data samples: " + str(len(imgPaths)))
    print("Number of Classes: " + str(numLabels))

    newShape = [(256,256,3)]
    destDir = ['/deeplearning-keras/ch05/data/resized_imgs']

    for newImgShape, destFolder in zip(newShape,destDir):
        for i, path,label in zip(count(),imgPaths,labels):
```

```
                split_path = path.split('/')
                newPath = 'size'+str(newImgShape[0])+'_'+split_path[-1]
                newPath = '/'.join([destFolder]+split_path[8:-1]+[newPath])
                add_flip = True
                if label == 1:
                    add_flip = False

                # Used to exclude corrupt data
                try:
                    resizeImage(path, maxSize=newImgShape, savePath=newPath,
    addFlip=add_flip)
                except OSError:
                    print("Error at path " + path)
```

The output will be as follows:

```
Using TensorFlow backend.
('Count of type1 : ', 250)
('Count of type2 : ', 781)
('Count of type3 : ', 450)
Total Number of data samples: 1481
Number of Classes: 3
```

1. Neural networks need the image size to be constant. Another consideration is that the images need to be small enough to leave enough RAM space for the model to train, but large enough that important characteristics are distinguishable for classification. We semi-arbitrarily chose 256 x 256 pixels for the image size.

2. The following function resizes the images while maintaining their aspect ratio:

```
# Image resizing is important considering memory footprint, but its
important to maintain key #characteristics that will preserve the
key features.
def resizeImage(imgPath, maxSize=(256,256,3), savePath=None,
addFlip=False):
    ImageFile.LOAD_TRUNCATED_IMAGES = True
    img = Image.open(imgPath)

    # set aspect ratio
    if type(img) == type(np.array([])):
        img = Image.fromarray(img)
    img.thumbnail(maxSize, Image.ANTIALIAS)
    tmpImage = (np.random.random(maxSize)*255).astype(np.uint8)
    resizedImg = Image.fromarray(tmpImage)
    resizedImg.paste(img, ((maxSize[0]-img.size[0])//2, (maxSize[1]-
img.size[1])//2))
```

```
    if savePath:
        resizedImg.save(savePath)

    if addFlip:
        flip = resizedImg.transpose(Image.FLIP_LEFT_RIGHT)
        if savePath:
            splitPath = savePath.split('/')
            flip_path = '/'.join(splitPath[:-1] +
['flipped_'+splitPath[-1]])
            flip.save(flip_path)
        return np.array(resizedImg, dtype=np.float32),
np.array(flip,dtype=np.float32)
    return np.array(resizedImg, dtype=np.float32)
```

Resized images are stored under the `resized_imgs` directory, as shown in the following screenshot:

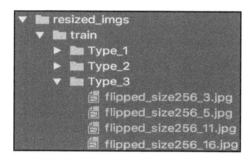

3. The next phase in the recipe is to train the CNN on the training dataset. As part of the cervical training, we read in the resized image paths to be used for the rest of the project:

```
resizedImageDir = ['/deeplearning-
keras/ch05/data/resized_imgs/train']

imagePaths = []
labels = []
for i, resizedPath in enumerate(resizedImageDir):
    new_paths, new_labels, n_classes = readFilePaths(resizedPath)
    if len(new_paths) > 0:
        imagePaths += new_paths
        labels += new_labels

imagePaths, labels = shuffle(imagePaths, labels)
```

4. We now split the data into training and validation sets. The training dataset is used to fit the model and the validation dataset is used to provide an unbiased evaluation of the model fit on the training dataset while tuning model hyperparameters. 80% of the data is for training and the other 20% is for validation. After splitting the data, we save the paths and labels to CSVs denoting which dataset they belong to; this ensures that the two datasets do not get mixed after being established:

```
trainCSV = '/deeplearning-keras/ch05/csvs/train_set.csv'
validCSV = '/deeplearning-keras/ch05/csvs/valid_set.csv'

training_portion = .8
split_index = int(training_portion * len(imagePaths))
X_train_paths, y_train = imagePaths[:split_index],
labels[:split_index]
X_valid_paths, y_valid = imagePaths[split_index:],
labels[split_index:]

print("Train size: ")
print(len(X_train_paths))
print("Valid size: ")
print(len(X_valid_paths))

savePaths(trainCSV, X_train_paths, y_train)
savePaths(validCSV, X_valid_paths, y_valid)

train_csv = 'csvs/train_set.csv'
valid_csv = 'csvs/valid_set.csv'

X_train_paths, y_train = getSplitData(train_csv)
X_valid_paths, y_valid = getSplitData(valid_csv)
n_classes = max(y_train) + 1
```

Data is separated into training and validation sets, X_train_paths and X_valid_paths, as the output of the previous code.

5. Now, we use one-hot encoding to represent categorical variables as binary vectors. A one-hot vector represents the label of a data sample as a vector of zeros with a single 1 value. The index of the 1 value corresponds to the label. One-hot encoding is a useful representation of the truth labels because it is an easy format to produce from the neural net. This makes the loss easy to calculate and propagate backward:

```
Y_train = oneHotEncode(y_train, n_classes)
y_valid = oneHotEncode(y_valid, n_classes)
```

6. The one-hot function is described in the following code snippet:

```
# one hot encoding
def oneHotEncode(labels, n_classes):
    one_hots = []
    for label in labels:
        one_hot = [0]*n_classes
        if label >= len(one_hot):
            print("Labels out of bounds\nCheck your n_classes
parameter")
            return
        one_hot[label] = 1
        one_hots.append(one_hot)
    return np.array(one_hots,dtype=np.float32)
```

7. Since there are too many images to be able to read all of them into memory as NumPy arrays, we create a generator to read the images into memory in batches. This will add random augmentations to effectively increase the size of our dataset:

```
batch_size = 110
add_random_augmentations = False
resize_dims = None
n_train_samples = len(X_train_paths)
train_steps_per_epoch = getSteps(n_train_samples, batch_size,
n_augs=1)
n_valid_samples = len(X_valid_paths)
valid_steps_per_epoch = getSteps(n_valid_samples, batch_size,
n_augs=0)
train_generator = image_generator(X_train_paths, y_train,
batch_size,
                                  resize_dims=resize_dims,
randomly_augment=add_random_augmentations)
valid_generator = image_generator(X_valid_paths, y_valid,
batch_size,
                                  resize_dims=resize_dims,
rand_order=False)
```

Modeling

The following diagram describes an input to the neural network, which runs through many layers (including **Convolutions**, **Subsampling**, and **Fully connected**), before finally getting to the results:

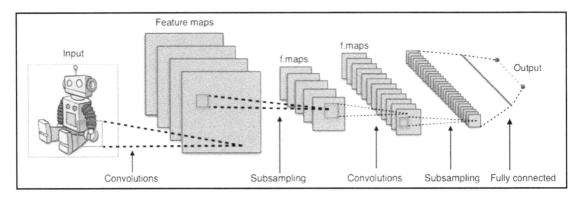

We create the model with two fully connected layers, decreasing in size, followed by an output layer. As convModel describes, we run 3 x 3, 4 x 4, and 5 x 5 filters in parallel at the first layer. For the following convolutional layers, we run 3 x 3 and 5 x 5 filters with decreasing depths due to RAM limits.

In Keras, we can just stack up layers by adding the desired layers one by one. That's exactly what we'll do here. In convModel, the depths of every layer are sequentially reduced. The stack of layers used is input, batch normalization, convolution, max pooling, dropout, **exponential linear unit** (**ELU**), and softmax. It is important to use dropout after max pooling because the dropout will have a more intense effect. This is because the effects of dropout can potentially go unnoticed if done before a max pooling layer.

ELU activations were chosen due to their protection against dead neurons.

1. We will be creating the CNN model first:

```
def convModel(first_conv_shapes=[(4,4),(3,3),(5,5)],
conv_shapes=[(3,3),(5,5)], conv_depths=[12,12,11,8,8],
dense_shapes=[100,50,3], image_shape=(256,256,3), n_labels=3):
    stacks = []
    pooling_filter = (2,2)
    pooling_stride = (2,2)
```

```
inputs = Input(shape=image_shape)
zen_layer = BatchNormalization()(inputs)

for shape in first_conv_shapes:
    stacks.append(Conv2D(conv_depths[0], shape, padding='same',
activation='elu')(zen_layer))
layer = concatenate(stacks,axis=-1)
layer = BatchNormalization()(layer)
layer =
MaxPooling2D(pooling_filter,strides=pooling_stride,padding='same')(
layer)
layer = Dropout(0.05)(layer)

for i in range(1,len(conv_depths)):
    stacks = []
    for shape in conv_shapes:
stacks.append(Conv2D(conv_depths[i],shape,padding='same',activation
='elu')(layer))
    layer = concatenate(stacks,axis=-1)
    layer = BatchNormalization()(layer)
    layer = Dropout(i*10**-2+.05)(layer)
    layer = MaxPooling2D(pooling_filter,strides=pooling_stride,
padding='same')(layer)

layer = Flatten()(layer)
fclayer = Dropout(0.1)(layer)

for i in range(len(dense_shapes)-1):
    fclayer = Dense(dense_shapes[i], activation='elu')(fclayer)
    fclayer = BatchNormalization()(fclayer)

outs = Dense(dense_shapes[-1], activation='softmax')(fclayer)

return inputs, outs
```

2. We now use the preceding `convModel` to fit on the training set. The **adaptive moment estimation** (**Adam**) optimizer is used as an optimization algorithm, which helps us to minimize an objective function. The Adam optimizer is a combination of RMSProp and momentum, with the advantages of low memory requirements and little need for tuning of the hyperparameters.

3. We keep a learning rate of `.001`. If the learning rate is set very low, training will progress slowly, as you are making very small updates to the weights. But if our learning rate is kept too high, it can cause unwanted divergent behavior in our loss function.

4. We use the `categorical_crossentropy` loss function, which measures the performance of a classification model and accuracy as metrics for measuring the performance of our model:

```
'''
modeling
'''
n_classes = 3
image_shape = (256, 256, 3)

first_conv_shapes = [(4, 4), (3, 3), (5, 5)]
conv_shapes = [(3, 3), (5, 5)]
conv_depths = [12, 12, 11, 8, 8]
dense_shapes = [100, 50, n_classes]

inputs, outs = convModel(first_conv_shapes, conv_shapes,
conv_depths, dense_shapes, image_shape, n_classes)

model = Model(inputs=inputs, outputs=outs)

learning_rate = .0001
for i in range(20):
    if i > 4:
        learning_rate = .00001   # Anneals the learning rate
    adam_opt = optimizers.Adam(lr=learning_rate)
    model.compile(loss='categorical_crossentropy',
optimizer=adam_opt, metrics=['accuracy'])
    history = model.fit_generator(train_generator,
train_steps_per_epoch, epochs=1,
                                  validation_data=valid_generator,
validation_steps=valid_steps_per_epoch, max_queue_size=1)
    model.save('/deeplearning-keras/ch05/weights/model.h5')
```

The output will be as follows, using the TensorFlow backend:

```
Train size:
1744
Valid size:
437
2018-09-10 06:58:45.775834: I
tensorflow/core/platform/cpu_feature_guard.cc:141] Your CPU
supports instructions that this TensorFlow binary was not compiled
to use: SSE4.1 SSE4.2 AVX AVX2 FMA
Epoch 1/1
1/32 [..............................] - ETA: 1:16:46 - loss: 2.0438
-
acc: 0.2545
2/32 [>.............................] - ETA: 1:11:16 - loss: 1.9240
```

```
- acc: 0.2727
3/32 [=>............................] - ETA: 1:08:00 - loss: 1.7749
- acc: 0.3091
4/32 [==>...........................] - ETA: 1:04:49 - loss: 1.7584
- acc: 0.2909
5/32 [===>..........................] - ETA: 1:01:39 - loss: 1.7117
-acc: 0.3109
6/32 [====>.........................] - ETA: 59:20 - loss: 1.6633 -
acc: 0.3303
7/32 [=====>........................] - ETA: 56:58 - loss: 1.6607 -
acc: 0.3221
8/32 [======>.......................] - ETA: 54:33 - loss: 1.6422 -
acc: 0.3239
9/32 [=======>......................] - ETA: 52:12 - loss: 1.6201 -
acc: 0.3222
10/32 [========>.....................] - ETA: 49:50 - loss: 1.6187
- acc: 0.3245
11/32 [=========>....................] - ETA: 47:38 - loss: 1.6232
- acc: 0.3223
12/32 [==========>...................] - ETA: 45:13 - loss: 1.6029
- acc: 0.3242
13/32 [==========>...................] - ETA: 42:55 - loss: 1.5900
- acc: 0.3224
14/32 [===========>..................] - ETA: 40:39 - loss: 1.5931
- acc: 0.3234
15/32 [=============>.................] - ETA: 38:19 - loss: 1.5896
- acc: 0.3261
16/32 [==============>................] - ETA: 35:41 - loss: 1.5790
- acc: 0.3309
17/32 [==============>................] - ETA: 33:25 - loss: 1.5626
- acc: 0.3345
18/32 [===============>...............] - ETA: 31:10 - loss: 1.5478
- acc: 0.3366
19/32 [================>..............] - ETA: 28:58 - loss: 1.5372
- acc: 0.3356
20/32 [=================>.............] - ETA: 26:45 - loss: 1.5302
- acc: 0.3366


1/32 [..............................] - ETA: 1:11:06 - loss: 0.8727
- acc: 0.6182
2/32 [>.............................] - ETA: 1:06:38 - loss: 0.8982
- acc: 0.6091
3/32 [=>............................] - ETA: 1:00:23 - loss: 0.8490
- acc: 0.6259
4/32 [==>...........................] - ETA: 58:48 - loss: 0.8642 -
acc: 0.6172
5/32 [===>..........................] - ETA: 56:59 - loss: 0.8392 -
```

```
                acc: 0.6210
                6/32 [====>........................] - ETA: 54:59 - loss: 0.8635 -
                acc: 0.6008
                7/32 [=====>.......................] - ETA: 52:57 - loss: 0.8610 -
                acc: 0.6020
                8/32 [======>......................] - ETA: 50:59 - loss: 0.8534 -
                acc: 0.5972
                3/32 [=>...........................] - ETA: 57:34 - loss: 0.8460 -
                acc: 0.6289
```

The model performs with an approximate **62% accuracy** on the validation set.

Predictions

As the last step, we perform predictions on the `test` dataset. We load the model and read in the test image paths. We then create a separate process for reading in and resizing the test images using `ThreadPool`. This allows the images to be processed while the model evaluates the samples. Predictions are stored in the predictions CSV file for evaluation:

```
'''
get predictions
'''
data_path = '/deeplearning-keras/ch05/data/test'
model_path = '/deeplearning-keras/ch05/weights/model.h5'

resize_dims = (256, 256, 3)
test_divisions = 20  # Used for segmenting image evaluation in threading
batch_size = 100  # Batch size used for keras predict function

ins, outs = convModel()
model = Model(inputs=ins, outputs=outs)
model.load_weights(model_path)
test_paths, test_labels, _ = readFilePaths(data_path, no_labels=True)
print(str(len(test_paths)) + ' testing images')

pool = ThreadPool(processes=1)
portion = len(test_paths) // test_divisions + 1  # Number of images to read
in per pool

async_result = pool.apply_async(convertImages, (test_paths[0 *
portion:portion * (0 + 1)],
                                                test_labels[0 *
portion:portion * (0 + 1)], resize_dims))

total_base_time = time.time()
test_imgs = []
```

```
predictions = []
for i in range(1, test_divisions + 1):
    base_time = time.time()

    print("Begin set " + str(i))
    while len(test_imgs) == 0:
        test_imgs, _ = async_result.get()
    img_holder = test_imgs
    test_imgs = []

    if i < test_divisions:
        async_result = pool.apply_async(convertImages, (test_paths[i *
portion:portion * (i + 1)],
                                                        test_labels[0 *
portion:portion * (0 + 1)],
                                                        resize_dims))

    predictions.append(model.predict(img_holder, batch_size=batch_size,
verbose=0))
    print("Execution Time: " + str((time.time() - base_time) / 60) +
'min\n')

predictions = np.concatenate(predictions, axis=0)
print("Total Execution Time: " + str((time.time() - total_base_time) / 60)
+ 'mins')

conf = .95  # Prediction confidence
savePredictions = '/deeplearning-keras/ch05/predictions.csv'
predictions = confid(predictions, conf)
header = 'image_name,Type_1,Type_2,Type_3'
save(savePredictions, test_labels, predictions, header)
```

The output will be as follows:

```
image_name,Type_1,Type_2,Type_3
63.jpg, 0.025,0.025,0.95
189.jpg, 0.025,0.95,0.025
77.jpg, 0.025,0.025,0.95
162.jpg, 0.025,0.025,0.95
176.jpg, 0.025,0.025,0.95
88.jpg, 0.025,0.95,0.025
348.jpg, 0.025,0.025,0.95
```

Digit recognition

The digit recognition MNIST dataset was developed by Yann LeCun, Corinna Cortes, and Christopher Burges for assessing machine learning models on the handwritten digit problem. Digit images were taken from a mixture of scanned documents, normalized in size, and centered. Each image is 28 pixels in height and 28 pixels in width, for a total of 784 pixels in total. Each pixel has a single pixel value associated with it, indicating the lightness or darkness of that pixel, with higher numbers meaning darker. This pixel value is an integer between 0 and 255, inclusive. We develop a digit recognition pipeline. We have 10 digits (0 to 9), or 10 classes, to predict.

Getting ready

In this recipe, we develop a modeling pipeline that tries to recognize a digit (0-9) based on images with greater accuracy. The modeling pipelines use CNN models written using the Keras functional API for image classification.

The Keras library provides a simple method for loading the MNIST data. The dataset is downloaded automatically into the user's home directory as the `mnist.pkl.gz` (15 MB) file:

```
from keras.datasets import mnist
# get dataset
(XTrain, yTrain), (XTest, yTest) = mnist.load_data()
```

We can see that downloading and loading the MNIST dataset is as easy as calling the `mnist.load_data()` function:

```
# plot 4 images as gray scale
plt.subplot(221)
plt.imshow(XTrain[1], cmap=plt.get_cmap('gray'))
plt.subplot(222)
plt.imshow(XTrain[2], cmap=plt.get_cmap('gray'))
plt.subplot(223)
plt.imshow(XTrain[3], cmap=plt.get_cmap('gray'))
plt.subplot(224)
plt.imshow(XTrain[4], cmap=plt.get_cmap('gray'))
# show the plot
plt.show()
```

Running the preceding code shows us the following digits.

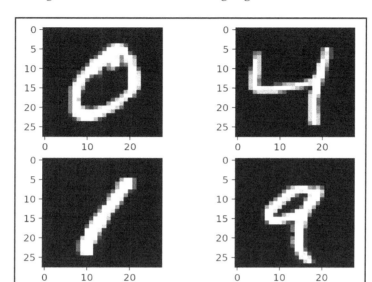

How to do it...

Let's create a simple CNN for the MNIST dataset that explains how to use all of the aspects of a CNN implementation, including the convolutional layers, pooling layers, and dropout layers. CNNs reduce the dimensions of the layers as we go deeper and increase the number of feature maps to detect more features and decrease the computational cost:

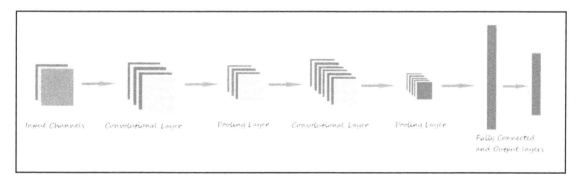

Let's import the required APIs:

```
import numpy
from keras import backend as K
from keras.utils import np_utils
from keras.layers import Dense, Flatten, Dropout
from keras.layers.convolutional import Conv2D, MaxPooling2D
from keras.models import Sequential
import matplotlib.pyplot as plt
from keras.datasets import mnist
from keras.layers.core import Activation
```

Modeling

1. Firstly, let's initialize the random number generator to a constant seed value for reproducibility of results:

   ```
   numpy.random.seed(0)
   ```

2. Keras sequential layers are stacked so that every layer transfers its output to the next layer without defining additional data; let's import `Sequential` from the models:

   ```
   # create sequential model
   model = Sequential()
   ```

3. To improve the efficiency and the convergence of the algorithm, we normalize the data based on the fact that the maximum pixel value is 255, so we divide all the pixels by 255 to obtain results between 0 and 1:

   ```
   # normalize the dataset
   XTrain = XTrain / 255
   XTest = XTest / 255
   ```

4. Exploring the data is an important aspect for choosing the right algorithm and getting the accuracy metric we need to use. If the data is balanced with class distribution we can easily use accuracy, but if the data is skewed, then we won't be able to use accuracy, as its results will be misleading and we should use another score mechanism:

```
# data exploration
print("Number of training examples = %i" % XTrain.shape[0])
print("Number of classes = %i" % len(numpy.unique(yTrain)))
print("Dimension of images = {:d} x {:d}
".format(XTrain[1].shape[0], XTrain[1].shape[1]))
unique, count = numpy.unique(yTrain, return_counts=True)
print("The number of occurrences of each class in the dataset = %s
" % dict(zip(unique, count)), "\n")
```

5. This is the output:

```
Number of training examples = 60000
Number of classes = 10
Dimension of images = 28 x 28
The number of occurrences of each class in the dataset = {0: 5923,
1: 6742, 2: 5958, 3: 6131, 4: 5842, 5: 5421, 6: 5918, 7: 6265, 8:
5851, 9: 5949}
```

Here, we can see that the dataset consists of 60,000 training samples, where each is an image with dimensions of 28 x 28. Since class distribution is balanced, we will use accuracy as the metric.

6. We reshape the data samples or images, in this case, so that they are suitable for training using a CNN API. In the `keras` library, the layers use pixel values with the dimensions as *(pixels) (width) (height)*. In the case of MNIST, where the pixel values are grayscale, the pixel dimension is set to 1.

7. We should also make the output in the form of one-hot encoding, which means that we will have 10 classes from 0 to 9, one class for each number:

```
XTrain = XTrain.reshape(XTrain.shape[0], 28, 28,
1).astype('float32')
XTest = XTest.reshape(XTest.shape[0], 28, 28, 1).astype('float32')
yTrain = np_utils.to_categorical(yTrain)
yTest = np_utils.to_categorical(yTest)
```

8. Let's now implement the first layer of the CNN with a simplistic architecture. For the sequential model, we will stack the layers and specify the images' input dimensions in the first layer, where the first layer will be a convolutional layer `Conv2D()`, specifying the number of feature maps, the input shape and the activation function, which is `relu`, in this case. We later add the max pooling layer with a kernel of dimensions 2 x 2:

```
# modeling
model.add(Conv2D(40, kernel_size=5, padding="same",
input_shape=(28, 28, 1), activation='relu'))
model.add(Conv2D(50, kernel_size=5, padding="valid",
activation='relu'))
model.add(MaxPooling2D(pool_size=(2, 2), strides=(2, 2)))
model.add(Dropout(0.2))
```

9. We then add a flatten layer that receives the output of the CNN and flattens it, passing it then as an input to the dense layers, which further more pass it to the output layer. We will use `softmax` with the output layer to output the expected probability vector for multiclass classification:

```
model.add(Flatten())
model.add(Dense(100))
model.add(Activation("relu"))
model.add(Dropout(0.2))
model.add(Dense(10))
model.add(Activation("softmax"))
```

10. We finally compile the model and train it using the `fit()` method, which fits the training data and classes, the number of epochs, and `batch_size`, which is the number of images per training cycle. As the last step, we evaluate the model to ensure that it doesn't overfit the training data. Evaluating the model is done by using the weights that resulted from the training step to predict the value of the test dataset, which the model hasn't seen before, to determine how well the model will perform on the unseen dataset. We use `categorical_crossentropy` as the cost function for that model, but what do we mean by the cost function? You can find it in the following snippet:

```
model.compile(loss='categorical_crossentropy', optimizer='adam',
metrics=['accuracy'])
model.fit(XTrain, yTrain, epochs=32, batch_size=200,
validation_split=0.2)
scores = model.evaluate(XTest, yTest, verbose=10)
print(scores)
```

11. Following is the output that was obtained by training 48,000 samples and was validated on 12,000 samples:

```
200/48000 [..............................] - ETA: 33:31 - loss:
2.3074 - acc: 0.0650
400/48000 [..............................] - ETA: 32:15 - loss:
2.2640 - acc: 0.1350
600/48000 [..............................] - ETA: 32:12 - loss:
2.2285 - acc: 0.1600
800/48000 [..............................] - ETA: 32:40 - loss:
2.1714 - acc: 0.1975
1000/48000 [..............................] - ETA: 33:09 - loss:
2.0927 - acc: 0.2650
48000/48000 [==============================] - 2382s 50ms/step -
loss: 0.2471 - acc: 0.9238
...
...
47600/48000 [==============================] - ETA: 17s - loss:
0.0067 - acc: 0.9978
47800/48000 [==============================] - ETA: 8s - loss: 0.0068
- acc: 0.9977
48000/48000 [==============================] - 2237s 47ms/step -
loss: 0.0069 - acc: 0.9977
```

We can run this network on a CPU. You should be able to see the preceding output. With a simple architecture, it achieves an accuracy of 99~.

6
Generative Adversarial Networks

In this chapter, we will cover the following points:

- Basic GAN
- Boundary seeking
- GAN DCGAN

Introduction

Generative adversarial networks (GANs) are one of the recent developments in deep learning. GANs were introduced by Ian Goodfellow in 2014 (`https://arxiv.org/pdf/1406.2661.pdf`). They address the problem of unsupervised learning by training two deep networks simultaneously, called a **generator** and a **discriminator**. These networks compete and cooperate with each other. Over the training period, both the networks eventually learn how to perform their tasks with better accuracy.

A GAN is almost always compared to the role of a counterfeiter (generator) and the police (discriminator). Initially, the counterfeiter will show the police fake money. The police say it is fake. The police give feedback to the counterfeiter as to why the money is fake. The counterfeiter tries to make new fake money based on the feedback they receive. The police again state the money is still fake and offer some more feedback. The counterfeiter makes another attempt, based on the latest feedback. This cycle continues indefinitely until the police are no longer able to detect the fake money because it looks real.

In this chapter, we will describe various recipes for GANs.

GAN overview

The adversarial modeling framework is straightforward to apply when the models are both multilayer perceptrons. To learn the generator's distribution p_g over data x, we define a prior on input noise variables $p(z)$. This is followed by representing mapping to data space as $G(Z, \theta_g)$, where G is a differentiable function represented by a multilayer perceptron with parameters θ_g. We also define a second multilayer perceptron called **discriminator**: $D(x, \theta_g)$ outputs a single scalar. $D(x)$ represents the probability that x came from the data rather than P_g. The objective is to train D to maximize the probability of assigning the correct label to both training examples and samples from G. We simultaneously train G to minimize $Log(1-D(G(Z)))$:

$$min_G max_D V(D, G) = \mathbb{E}_{x \sim p_{data}(x)}[log D(x)] + \mathbb{E}_{z \sim p_z(z)}[log(1 - D(G(z)))]$$

Basic GAN

In this recipe, we look at the most basic GAN network for the Fashion-MNIST dataset.

Fashion-MNIST is a dataset of Zalando article images consisting of a training set of 60,000 examples; it also contains a test set of 10,000 examples. Each example is a 28 x 28 grayscale image, associated with a label from 10 classes.

Here are some example images from Fashion-MNIST:

Fashion MNIST is directly available in Keras.

Getting ready

Create a class called **GAN**. Import the relevant classes and initialize the variables:

```
from __future__ import print_function, division
from keras.datasets import fashion_mnist
from keras.layers import Input, Dense, Reshape, Flatten, Dropout
from keras.layers import BatchNormalization, Activation, ZeroPadding2D
from keras.layers.advanced_activations import LeakyReLU
from keras.layers.convolutional import UpSampling2D, Conv2D
from keras.models import Sequential, Model
from keras.optimizers import Adam
import matplotlib.pyplot as plt
import sys
import numpy as np

GAN class():
....
```

Define the constants to be used in the _init_() method of the program:

```
self.img_rows = 28
 self.img_cols = 28
 self.channels = 1
 self.img_shape = (self.img_rows, self.img_cols, self.channels)
 self.latent_dim = 100
```

Note the `img_shape` is `(28,28,1)` and `latent_dim` is `100`.

How to do it...

The GAN network for the Fashion-MNIST dataset is explained in the following sections:

Building a generator

We create a sequential model with the following layers:

- Dense layer with an input of (`self.latent_dim`) and output of (*, 256 units)
- The leaky ReLU layer applies this function to incoming data
- Batch normalization: normalizes the data
- Dense layer of 512: layer with output of (*, 512 units)

- Batch normalization
- Dense layer of (*, 1024)
- Leaky RELU
- Batch normalization
- Dense layer of size (*, 256) with activation `tanh`
- Reshape back to `img_shape`
- Add some noise to the model of type `shape=(self.latent_dim,)`:

```
def build_generator(self):
model = Sequential()
model.add(Dense(256, input_dim=self.latent_dim))
model.add(LeakyReLU(alpha=0.2))
model.add(BatchNormalization(momentum=0.8))
model.add(Dense(512))
model.add(LeakyReLU(alpha=0.2))
model.add(BatchNormalization(momentum=0.8))
model.add(Dense(1024))
model.add(LeakyReLU(alpha=0.2))
model.add(BatchNormalization(momentum=0.8))
model.add(Dense(np.prod(self.img_shape), activation='tanh'))
model.add(Reshape(self.img_shape))
model.summary()
noise = Input(shape=(self.latent_dim,))
img = model(noise)
return Model(noise, img)
```

Let's look at how the noise is transformed into an image in the generator:

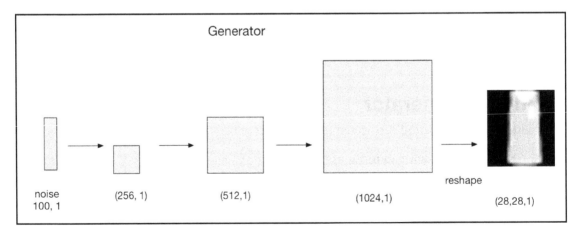

A model summary is listed in the following code snippet:

```
Layer (type) Output Shape Param #
=================================================================
dense_4 (Dense) (None, 256) 25856

leaky_re_lu_3 (LeakyReLU) (None, 256) 0

batch_normalization_1 (Batch (None, 256) 1024

dense_5 (Dense) (None, 512) 131584

leaky_re_lu_4 (LeakyReLU) (None, 512) 0

batch_normalization_2 (Batch (None, 512) 2048

dense_6 (Dense) (None, 1024) 525312

leaky_re_lu_5 (LeakyReLU) (None, 1024) 0

batch_normalization_3 (Batch (None, 1024) 4096

dense_7 (Dense) (None, 784) 803600

reshape_1 (Reshape) (None, 28, 28, 1) 0
=================================================================
Total params: 1,493,520
Trainable params: 1,489,936
Non-trainable params: 3,584
```

Building a discriminator

A discriminator can also be made into a sequential model by going in the opposite direction:

- The first layer is to flatten the `input_shape` of 28,28,1
- Add a dense layer with an output (*, 512)
- Add an activation function of Leaky ReLU
- Add another dense layer, which outputs (*, 256)
- Add another activation function of leaky ReLU

- Add a final output of (*, 1):

```
def build_discriminator(self):
    model = Sequential()
    model.add(Flatten(input_shape=self.img_shape))
    model.add(Dense(512))
    model.add(LeakyReLU(alpha=0.2))
    model.add(Dense(256))
    model.add(LeakyReLU(alpha=0.2))
    model.add(Dense(1, activation='sigmoid'))
    model.summary()
    img = Input(shape=self.img_shape)
    validity = model(img)
    return Model(img, validity)
```

Initialize the GAN instance

We created a custom GAN class, which is initialized with a generator and a discriminator. The steps followed are listed in the following points:

1. Initialize the variables `img_rows`, `img_cols`, `channels`, `img_shape`, and `latent_dim`.
2. Initialize the `optimizer`; we are using the Adam optimizer in this case.
3. Instantiate the discriminator:
    - Use `build_discriminator()`
    - Compile the discriminator with the `loss` function as `binary_crossentropy`, the optimizer as Adam, and the metrics as accuracy
4. Generator:
    - Instantiate using `build_generator()`
    - Get the generated image with noise as input
5. Discriminator checks the validity of the images
6. Combined model: used to fool the discriminator with the generator:
    - z with the input shape (`*, self.latent_dim`) is the input to the generator
    - The generator's output is the input to the discriminator

7. Compile the `loss` of the combined model:

```
def __init__(self):
    self.img_rows = 28
    self.img_cols = 28
    self.channels = 1
    self.img_shape = (self.img_rows, self.img_cols, self.channels)
    self.latent_dim = 100
    optimizer = Adam(0.0002, 0.5)
    # Build and compile the discriminator
    self.discriminator = self.build_discriminator()
    self.discriminator.compile(loss='binary_crossentropy',
        optimizer=optimizer,
        metrics=['accuracy'])
    # Build the generator
    self.generator = self.build_generator()
    # The generator takes noise as input and generates imgs
    z = Input(shape=(self.latent_dim,))
    img = self.generator(z)
    # For the combined model we will only train the generator
    self.discriminator.trainable = False
    # The discriminator takes generated images as input and
determines validity
    validity = self.discriminator(img)
    # The combined model (stacked generator and discriminator)
    # Trains the generator to fool the discriminator
    self.combined = Model(z, validity)
    self.combined.compile(loss='binary_crossentropy',
optimizer=optimizer)
```

In the next section, we look at how to tie everything together and train the GAN iteratively, compile the losses, and store the generated images.

Training the GAN

Let's look at how the model is trained:

1. First, load the dataset
2. Rescale the data
3. Generate valid and fake ground truths

4. For each iteration of an epoch, do the following:
- Select a random batch of images
- Generate images
- Calculate the loss for real and fake images
- Sample and plot the images:

```
def train(self, epochs, batch_size=128,
sample_interval=50):

    # Load the dataset
    (X_train, _), (_, _) = fashion_mnist.load_data()

    # Rescale -1 to 1
    X_train = X_train / 127.5 - 1.
    X_train = np.expand_dims(X_train, axis=3)

    # Adversarial ground truths
    valid = np.ones((batch_size, 1))
    fake = np.zeros((batch_size, 1))

    for epoch in range(epochs):

        # ---------------------
        #  Train Discriminator
        # ---------------------

        # Select a random batch of images
        idx = np.random.randint(0, X_train.shape[0],
batch_size)
        imgs = X_train[idx]

        noise = np.random.normal(0, 1, (batch_size,
self.latent_dim))

        # Generate a batch of new images
        gen_imgs = self.generator.predict(noise)

        # Train the discriminator
        d_loss_real =
self.discriminator.train_on_batch(imgs, valid)
        d_loss_fake =
self.discriminator.train_on_batch(gen_imgs, fake)
        d_loss = 0.5 * np.add(d_loss_real, d_loss_fake)

        # ---------------------
        #  Train Generator
        # ---------------------
```

```
        noise = np.random.normal(0, 1, (batch_size,
self.latent_dim))

        # Train the generator (to have the discriminator
label samples as valid)
        g_loss = self.combined.train_on_batch(noise, valid)

        # Plot the progress
        print ("%d [D loss: %f, acc.: %.2f%%] [G loss: %f]"
% (epoch, d_loss[0], 100*d_loss[1], g_loss))

        # If at save interval => save generated image
samples
        if epoch % sample_interval == 0:
 self.sample_images(epoch)
```

Output plots

Let's start with the plot after the first iteration:

These are images after 9,000 iterations:

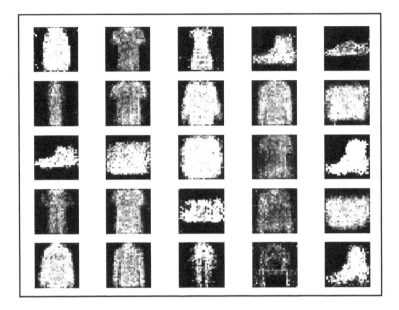

These are images after 29,800 iterations:

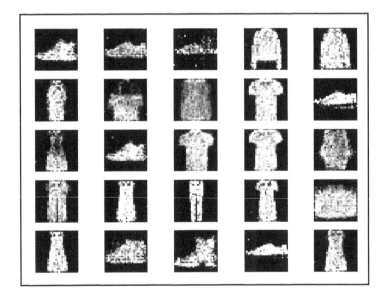

Average metrics of the GAN

After running the model for 30,000 iterations, the following metrics can be seen:

```
mean d loss:0.6404680597275333
 mean g loss:0.9513815407413333
 mean d accuracy:62.71046875
```

Mean discriminator loss is about 0.64 and generator loss is 0.95. Discriminator accuracy is about 62 percent. We also plotted the metrics as a function of epochs:

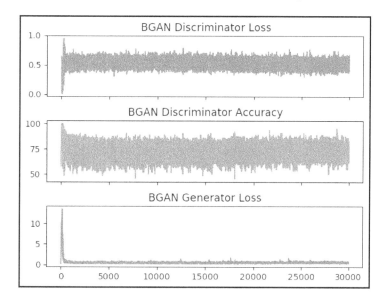

Next, let's look at a more advanced GAN called a **boundary seeking GAN**.

Boundary seeking GAN

Following the objective function shown here, in the original *GAN paper*:

$$min_G max_D V(D, G) = \mathbb{E}_{x \sim p_{data}(x)} [logD(x)] + \mathbb{E}_{z \sim p_z(z)} [log(1 - D(G(z)))]$$

Where:

- x: Data
- p_g: Generator's distribution over data x
- *p(z)*: A priori on input noise variable

- $G(Z,\theta_g)$: Map prior to data space
- G: Differentiable function represented by multi-layer perceptron with parameters θ_g
- $D(x,\theta_g)$: Discriminator-second multilayer perceptron which outputs a single scalar
- $D(x)$: The probability that x came from the data rather than p_g

The objective is to train D to maximize the probability of assigning the correct label to both training examples and samples from G. We simultaneously train G to minimize $Log(1-D(G(Z)))$; the optimal discriminator $D_G(X)$ is given by:

$$D_G^*(x) = \frac{p_{data}(x)}{p_{data}(x) + p_g(x)}$$

Where $p_{data}(x)$ is the real distribution, which can be found by rearranging the terms shown in the preceding example:

$$p_{data}(x) = p_g(x)\frac{D_G^*(x)}{1 - D_G^*(x)}$$

The assumption is that if we train $D(x)$ more and more, it will come closer and closer to $D_G(X)$ and our GAN training becomes better and better. For optimal generator, $p_{data}(x) = p_g(x)$, the optimal generator has a value of 0.5. Notice that $D(x) = 0.5$ is the decision boundary. We want to generate $x \sim G(x)$ such that it is near the decision boundary. Therefore, this method is called a boundary seeking GAN.

If we substitute $D(x) = 1 - D(x) = 0.5$, the objective function becomes as shown here:

$$\min_{G} \ \mathbb{E}_{z \sim p_z(z)} \left[\frac{1}{2}(\log D(x) - \log(1 - D(x)))^2\right]$$

We are taking a log of $D(x)$, as $D(x)$ is a probability distribution. In this recipe, we are going to look at how to implement a boundary seeking GAN in Keras.

Getting ready

Create a class called **BGAN**. Import the relevant classes and initialize the variables:

```
from __future__ import print_function, division

from keras.datasets import fashion_mnist
from keras.layers import Input, Dense, Reshape, Flatten, Dropout
from keras.layers import BatchNormalization, Activation, ZeroPadding2D
from keras.layers.advanced_activations import LeakyReLU
from keras.layers.convolutional import UpSampling2D, Conv2D
from keras.models import Sequential, Model
from keras.optimizers import Adam
import keras.backend as K
import matplotlib.pyplot as plt
import sys
import numpy as np

class BGAN():
....
```

Define the constants to be used in the program, as shown in the following listing:

```
self.img_rows = 28
self.img_cols = 28
self.channels = 1
self.img_shape = (self.img_rows, self.img_cols, self.channels)
self.latent_dim = 100
```

Note the `img_shape` is `(28,28,1)` and `latent_dim` is `100`.

How to do it...

Create a generator and discriminator, compare the loss, and iterate.

Generator

We create a sequential model with the following layers:

- Dense layer with an input of (`self.latent_dim`) and output of (*, 256 units)
- Leaky ReLU layer applies this function to incoming data
- Batch Normalization: normalizes the data

- Dense layer of 512: Layer with output of (*, 512 units)
- Leaky ReLU layer applies this function to incoming data
- Batch normalization
- Dense layer of (*, 1024)
- Leaky RELU
- Batch normalization
- Dense layer of size (*, 256) with activation `tanh`
- Reshape back to `img_shape`
- Add some noise to the model of type `shape=(self.latent_dim,):`

```
def build_generator(self):
    model = Sequential()
    model.add(Dense(256, input_dim=self.latent_dim))
    model.add(LeakyReLU(alpha=0.2))
    model.add(BatchNormalization(momentum=0.8))
    model.add(Dense(512))
    model.add(LeakyReLU(alpha=0.2))
    model.add(BatchNormalization(momentum=0.8))
    model.add(Dense(1024))
    model.add(LeakyReLU(alpha=0.2))
    model.add(BatchNormalization(momentum=0.8))
    model.add(Dense(np.prod(self.img_shape), activation='tanh'))
    model.add(Reshape(self.img_shape))
    model.summary()
    noise = Input(shape=(self.latent_dim,))
    img = model(noise)
    return Model(noise, img)
```

Next, let's look at the discriminator, which will check how close our images are to the real images.

Discriminator

A discriminator is also a sequential model going in the opposite direction:

- The first layer is to flatten `input_shape` of 28,28,1
- Add a dense layer with an output (*, 512)
- Add an activation function of leaky ReLU
- Add another dense layer which outputs (*, 256)

- Add another activation function of leaky ReLU
- Add a final output of (*, 1) with an activation of `sigmoid`:

```
def build_discriminator(self):
    model = Sequential()
    model.add(Flatten(input_shape=self.img_shape))
    model.add(Dense(512))
    model.add(LeakyReLU(alpha=0.2))
    model.add(Dense(256))
    model.add(LeakyReLU(alpha=0.2))
    model.add(Dense(1, activation='sigmoid'))
    model.summary()
    img = Input(shape=self.img_shape)
    validity = model(img)
    return Model(img, validity)
```

In the next section, we look at how to initialize the BGAN class.

Initializing the BGAN class

We created a custom class GAN, which is initialized with a generator and a discriminator. The steps followed are listed in the following points:

1. Initialize the variables `img_rows`, `img_cols`, `channels`, `img_shape`, and `latent_dim`
2. Initialize the `optimizer`; we are using the Adam optimizer in this case
3. Instantiate the discriminator:
    - Use `build_discriminator()`
    - Compile the discriminator with the loss function as `binary_crossentropy`, the optimizer as Adam, and the metrics as accuracy
4. Generator:
    - Instantiate using `build_generator()`
    - Get the generated image with noise as the input
5. Discriminator checks the validity of the images
6. Combined model: Used to fool the discriminator with the generator:
    - z with input shape (`*, self.latent_dim`) is the input to the generator
    - Generator's output is the input to the discriminator

7. Compile the loss of the combined model. This is where it gets interesting; notice that we are using boundary seeking loss:

```
class BGAN():

    def __init__(self):
        self.img_rows = 28
        self.img_cols = 28
        self.channels = 1
        self.img_shape = (self.img_rows, self.img_cols,
self.channels)
        self.latent_dim = 100

        optimizer = Adam(0.0002, 0.5)

        # Build and compile the discriminator
        self.discriminator = self.build_discriminator()
        self.discriminator.compile(loss='binary_crossentropy',
            optimizer=optimizer,
            metrics=['accuracy'])

        # Build the generator
        self.generator = self.build_generator()

        # The generator takes noise as input and generated imgs
        z = Input(shape=(100,))
        img = self.generator(z)

        # For the combined model we will only train the generator
        self.discriminator.trainable = False

        # The valid takes generated images as input and determines
validity
        valid = self.discriminator(img)

        # The combined model (stacked generator and discriminator)
        # Trains the generator to fool the discriminator
        self.combined = Model(z, valid)
        self.combined.compile(loss=self.boundary_loss,
optimizer=optimizer)
```

Boundary seeking loss

Boundary seeking loss, as we explained in the section at the start of this recipe, is implemented with the following equation:

$$\min_{G} \; \mathbb{E}_{z \sim p_z(z)} \left[\frac{1}{2} (\log D(x) - \log(1 - D(x)))^2 \right]$$

Where $D(x)$ is the probability that x came from data rather than p_g.

Boundary seeking loss: See the following reference: `https://wiseodd.` `github.io/techblog/2017/03/07/boundary-seeking-gan/`.

This is the only major change compared to the previous sample. It is implemented in our class with the following function:

```
import keras.backend as K

def boundary_loss(self, y_true, y_pred):
    return 0.5 * K.mean((K.log(y_pred) - K.log(1 - y_pred))**2)
```

Next, we will look at how to train this network with the training dataset.

Train the BGAN

Let's look at how the model is trained:

1. First, load the dataset
2. Rescale the data
3. Generate valid and fake ground truths
4. For each iteration of an epoch, do the following:
   - Select a random batch of images
   - Generate images
   - Calculate loss for real and fake images

- Sample and plot the images:

```
def train(self, epochs, batch_size=128,
sample_interval=50):

    # Load the dataset
    (X_train, _), (_, _) = fashion_mnist.load_data()

    # Rescale -1 to 1
    X_train = X_train / 127.5 - 1.
    X_train = np.expand_dims(X_train, axis=3)

    # Adversarial ground truths
    valid = np.ones((batch_size, 1))
    fake = np.zeros((batch_size, 1))

    for epoch in range(epochs):

        # ---------------------
        #  Train Discriminator
        # ---------------------

        # Select a random batch of images
        idx = np.random.randint(0, X_train.shape[0],
batch_size)
        imgs = X_train[idx]

        noise = np.random.normal(0, 1, (batch_size,
self.latent_dim))

        # Generate a batch of new images
        gen_imgs = self.generator.predict(noise)

        # Train the discriminator
        d_loss_real =
self.discriminator.train_on_batch(imgs, valid)
        d_loss_fake =
self.discriminator.train_on_batch(gen_imgs, fake)
        d_loss = 0.5 * np.add(d_loss_real, d_loss_fake)


        # ---------------------
        #  Train Generator
        # ---------------------

        g_loss = self.combined.train_on_batch(noise, valid)

        # Plot the progress
```

```
        print ("%d [D loss: %f, acc.: %.2f%%] [G loss: %f]"
% (epoch, d_loss[0], 100*d_loss[1], g_loss))

        # If at save interval => save generated image
samples
        if epoch % sample_interval == 0:
            self.sample_images(epoch)
```

Output the plots

The sample plots are shown for various iterations.

Iteration 0

This is the sample image generated by the first iteration:

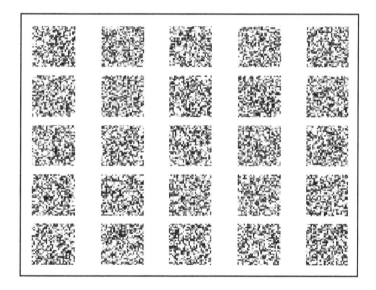

Iteration 10000

This shows the image generated for iteration 10000. Notice how the objects are clearer than with a simple GAN:

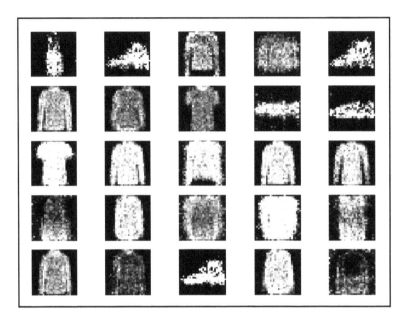

Metrics of the BGAN model

We calculated the mean `D loss`, `D accuracy`, and `G loss`. (Here **discriminator** (**D**) and **generator** (**G**)):

```
mean d loss:0.5253478690446334
mean g loss:0.5571205118226668
mean d accuracy:72.77859375
```

As can be seen, `d accuracy` is much higher than that of a simple GAN.

Plotting the metrics

Let's also plot the metrics we got the average values for earlier:

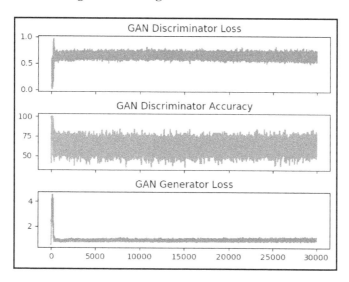

Generator loss starts at a very high value and settles down over a period of time.

DCGAN

CNNs for a GAN had been unsuccessful for some time until authors of the `paper()` came up with the following approach.

Here are the architecture guidelines for stable deep convolutional GANs:

- Replace any pooling layers with strided convolutions (discriminator) and fractional-strided convolutions (generator)
- Use batch norm in both the generator and the discriminator
- Remove fully connected hidden layers for deeper architectures
- Use ReLU activation in the generator for all layers except for the output, which uses `tanh`
- Use `LeakyReLU` activation in the discriminator for all layers

To build this architecture, we are going to use the same Fashion-MNIST dataset.

Getting ready

Make relevant imports and initialize the DCGAN class, as shown in the following code:

```
from __future__ import print_function, division

from keras.datasets import fashion_mnist
from keras.layers import Input, Dense, Reshape, Flatten, Dropout
from keras.layers import BatchNormalization, Activation, ZeroPadding2D
from keras.layers.advanced_activations import LeakyReLU
from keras.layers.convolutional import UpSampling2D, Conv2D
from keras.models import Sequential, Model
from keras.optimizers import Adam
import matplotlib.pyplot as plt
import sys
import numpy as np

class DCGAN():
    ...
```

Define the constants to be used later:

```
class DCGAN():
    def __init__(self):
        # Input shape
        self.img_rows = 28
        self.img_cols = 28
        self.channels = 1
        self.img_shape = (self.img_rows, self.img_cols, self.channels)
        self.latent_dim = 100
```

The rest of the logic we will look at in the following sections:

- Creating a generator
- Creating a discriminator
- Looping through the iterations and evaluating loss

How to do it...

Let's first look at the generator.

Generator

Creating a generator consists of implementing two layers of convolutional layers with leaky ReLU activations:

- Dense layer with output of (128*7*7)
- Reshape it to (7,7,128)
- Upsample 2D (upsampling refers to a technique that will upsamples an image to a higher resolution; 2D means upsample two 2D images)
- Convolution 2D with an output of 128 filters
- Batch normalization
- RELU activation
- Upsample 2D
- Convolution 2D with an output of 64 filters
- Batch normalization
- RELU activation
- Convolution 2D with an output of three filters
- Last activation of `tanh`:

```python
def build_generator(self):

    model = Sequential()
    model.add(Dense(128 * 7 * 7, activation="relu",
input_dim=self.latent_dim))
    model.add(Reshape((7, 7, 128)))
    model.add(UpSampling2D())
    model.add(Conv2D(128, kernel_size=3, padding="same"))
    model.add(BatchNormalization(momentum=0.8))
    model.add(Activation("relu"))
    model.add(UpSampling2D())
    model.add(Conv2D(64, kernel_size=3, padding="same"))
    model.add(BatchNormalization(momentum=0.8))
    model.add(Activation("relu"))
    model.add(Conv2D(self.channels, kernel_size=3, padding="same"))
    model.add(Activation("tanh"))
    model.summary()
    noise = Input(shape=(self.latent_dim,))
    img = model(noise)

    return Model(noise, img)
```

Summary of the generator

We start with a flat input, 633472, and finally output an image with shape (28, 28, 1):

```
Layer (type) Output Shape Param #
=================================================================
dense_2 (Dense) (None, 6272) 633472
_____
reshape_1 (Reshape) (None, 7, 7, 128) 0
_____
up_sampling2d_1 (UpSampling2 (None, 14, 14, 128) 0
_____
conv2d_5 (Conv2D) (None, 14, 14, 128) 147584
_____
batch_normalization_4 (Batch (None, 14, 14, 128) 512
_____
activation_1 (Activation) (None, 14, 14, 128) 0
_____
up_sampling2d_2 (UpSampling2 (None, 28, 28, 128) 0
_____
conv2d_6 (Conv2D) (None, 28, 28, 64) 73792
_____
batch_normalization_5 (Batch (None, 28, 28, 64) 256
_____
activation_2 (Activation) (None, 28, 28, 64) 0
_____
conv2d_7 (Conv2D) (None, 28, 28, 1) 577
_____
activation_3 (Activation) (None, 28, 28, 1) 0
=================================================================
Total params: 856,193
Trainable params: 855,809
Non-trainable params: 384
```

Training the generator

Training is done as part of the __init__(self) function. We will use the Adam optimizer:

1. First, we build the discriminator using build_discriminator()
2. Then, we call compile on self.discriminator with a loss function and binary_crossentropy, the previously defined optimizer, and metrics as accuracy:

```
def __init__(self):
    ....
```

```
optimizer = Adam(0.0002, 0.5)
# Build the generator
self.generator = self.build_generator()

# The generator takes noise as input and generates imgs
z = Input(shape=(100,))
img = self.generator(z)
```

Next, we will look at the discriminator.

Discriminator

Let's first look at how the discriminator is built.

Build the discriminator

The discriminator starts with the image and goes in the opposite direction, finally outputting the loss:

```
def build_discriminator(self):
    model = Sequential()
    model.add(Conv2D(32, kernel_size=3, strides=2,
input_shape=self.img_shape, padding="same"))
    model.add(LeakyReLU(alpha=0.2))
    model.add(Dropout(0.25))
    model.add(Conv2D(64, kernel_size=3, strides=2, padding="same"))
    model.add(ZeroPadding2D(padding=((0,1),(0,1))))
    model.add(BatchNormalization(momentum=0.8))
    model.add(LeakyReLU(alpha=0.2))
    model.add(Dropout(0.25))
    model.add(Conv2D(128, kernel_size=3, strides=2, padding="same"))
    model.add(BatchNormalization(momentum=0.8))
    model.add(LeakyReLU(alpha=0.2))
    model.add(Dropout(0.25))
    model.add(Conv2D(256, kernel_size=3, strides=1, padding="same"))
    model.add(BatchNormalization(momentum=0.8))
    model.add(LeakyReLU(alpha=0.2))
    model.add(Dropout(0.25))
    model.add(Flatten())
    model.add(Dense(1, activation='sigmoid'))
    model.summary()

    img = Input(shape=self.img_shape)
    validity = model(img)

    return Model(img, validity)
```

Summary of the discriminator

At runtime, the discriminator has the following summary:

```
Layer (type) Output Shape Param #
=================================================================
conv2d_1 (Conv2D) (None, 14, 14, 32) 320
_____
leaky_re_lu_1 (LeakyReLU) (None, 14, 14, 32) 0
_____
dropout_1 (Dropout) (None, 14, 14, 32) 0
_____
conv2d_2 (Conv2D) (None, 7, 7, 64) 18496
_____
zero_padding2d_1 (ZeroPaddin (None, 8, 8, 64) 0
_____
batch_normalization_1 (Batch (None, 8, 8, 64) 256
_____
leaky_re_lu_2 (LeakyReLU) (None, 8, 8, 64) 0
_____
dropout_2 (Dropout) (None, 8, 8, 64) 0
_____
conv2d_3 (Conv2D) (None, 4, 4, 128) 73856
_____
batch_normalization_2 (Batch (None, 4, 4, 128) 512
_____
leaky_re_lu_3 (LeakyReLU) (None, 4, 4, 128) 0
_____
dropout_3 (Dropout) (None, 4, 4, 128) 0
_____
conv2d_4 (Conv2D) (None, 4, 4, 256) 295168
_____
batch_normalization_3 (Batch (None, 4, 4, 256) 1024
_____
leaky_re_lu_4 (LeakyReLU) (None, 4, 4, 256) 0
_____
dropout_4 (Dropout) (None, 4, 4, 256) 0
_____
flatten_1 (Flatten) (None, 4096) 0
_____
dense_1 (Dense) (None, 1) 4097
=================================================================
Total params: 393,729
Trainable params: 392,833
Non-trainable params: 896
```

Compile the discriminator

The discriminator is compiled in the `__init__(self)` function, similar to the generator:

```
def __init__(self):
 ....
 optimizer = Adam(0.0002, 0.5)

 # Build and compile the discriminator
 self.discriminator = self.build_discriminator()
 self.discriminator.compile(loss='binary_crossentropy',
 optimizer=optimizer,
 metrics=['accuracy'])

 ...
 self.discriminator.trainable = False
    # The discriminator takes generated images as input and determines
validity
    valid = self.discriminator(img)
```

Combined model - generator and discriminator

In this section, we look at how we create a combined model, which is a combination of generator and discriminator, to make the generator better. The following code is in the `__init__(self)` function:

```
def __init__(self):
 ....
 optimizer = Adam(0.0002, 0.5)

 # Build and compile the discriminator
 self.discriminator = self.build_discriminator()
 self.discriminator.compile(loss='binary_crossentropy',
 optimizer=optimizer,
 metrics=['accuracy'])

 # Build the generator
 self.generator = self.build_generator()

 # The generator takes noise as input and generates imgs
 z = Input(shape=(100,))
 img = self.generator(z)

 # For the combined model we will only train the generator
    self.discriminator.trainable = False
```

```
    # The discriminator takes generated images as input and determines
validity
    valid = self.discriminator(img)

    # The combined model (stacked generator and discriminator)
    # Trains the generator to fool the discriminator
    self.combined = Model(z, valid)
    self.combined.compile(loss='binary_crossentropy', optimizer=optimizer)
```

The following diagram shows how the combined models stack up together:

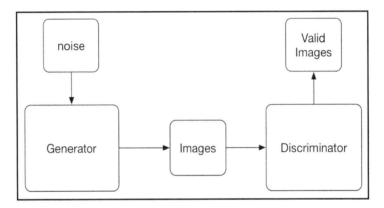

Train the generator using feedback from a discriminator

In this section, we look at how generator loss is calculated and the discriminator is made smarter by feeding it the loss between real and valid images:

- First, create adversarial ground truths: valid and fake image data holders
- Iterate over epochs:
    - Select a random set of images
    - Using noise, generate images using the generator
    - Use real images and valid images to calculate d_loss against fake and valid images
    - Calculate the total discriminator loss as an average

- Calculate the combined loss for generator and discriminator stacked on top of each other:

```
def train(self, epochs, batch_size=128, save_interval=50):

    # Load the dataset
    (X_train, _), (_, _) = fashion_mnist.load_data()

    # Rescale -1 to 1
    X_train = X_train / 127.5 - 1.
    X_train = np.expand_dims(X_train, axis=3)

    # Adversarial ground truths
    valid = np.ones((batch_size, 1))
    fake = np.zeros((batch_size, 1))

    for epoch in range(epochs):

        # ---------------------
        #  Train Discriminator
        # ---------------------

        # Select a random half of images
        idx = np.random.randint(0, X_train.shape[0],
batch_size)
        imgs = X_train[idx]

        # Sample noise and generate a batch of new images
        noise = np.random.normal(0, 1, (batch_size,
self.latent_dim))
        gen_imgs = self.generator.predict(noise)

        # Train the discriminator (real classified as ones
and generated as zeros)
        d_loss_real =
self.discriminator.train_on_batch(imgs, valid)
        d_loss_fake =
self.discriminator.train_on_batch(gen_imgs, fake)
        d_loss = 0.5 * np.add(d_loss_real, d_loss_fake)

        # ---------------------
        #  Train Generator
        # ---------------------

        # Train the generator (wants discriminator to
mistake images as real)
        g_loss = self.combined.train_on_batch(noise, valid)
```

```
                    # Plot the progress
                    print ("%d [D loss: %f, acc.: %.2f%%] [G loss: %f]"
        % (epoch, d_loss[0], 100*d_loss[1], g_loss))

                    # If at save interval => save generated image
        samples
                    if epoch % save_interval == 0:
                        self.save_imgs(epoch)
```

Putting it all together

In the `main` method, we instantiate the DCGAN class and call the `train` method:

```
if __name__ == '__main__':
    dcgan = DCGAN()
    dcgan.train(epochs=4000, batch_size=32, save_interval=50)
```

The output of the program

The output of the program after a few iterations is shown here.

This is the output for iteration 0:

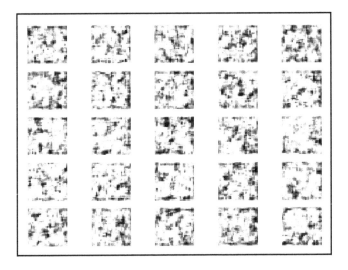

This is the output for iteration 100:

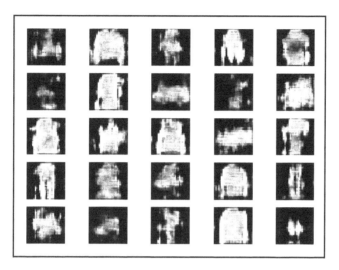

This is the output for iteration 1,500:

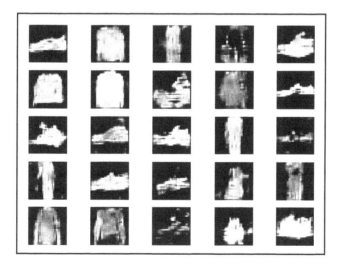

As can be seen in the preceding picture, it becomes clearer in a smaller number of iterations than a simple GAN or a boundary seeking GAN.

Average metrics of the model

We also calculated the model's `G loss`, `D loss`, and `D accuracy`:

```
mean d loss:0.6240914929024999
mean g loss:1.2823512871799998
mean d accuracy:65.574609375
```

Recurrent Neural Networks

7

In this chapter, we will cover the following recipes:

- Simple RNNs for time series data
- LSTM networks for time series data
- LSTM memory example time series forecasting with LSTM
- Sequence to sequence learning for the same length output with LSTM

Introduction

In this chapter, we will learn various recipes on how to create **recurrent neural networks** (**RNNs**) using Keras. First, we will understand the need for RNN. We will start with the simple RNNs followed by **long short-term memory** (**LSTM**) RNNs (these networks remember the state over a long period of time because of special gates in the cell).

The need for RNNs

Traditional neural networks cannot remember their past interactions, and that is a significant shortcoming. RNNs address this issue. They are networks with loops in them, allowing information to persist. RNNs have loops. In the next diagram, a chunk of the neural network, $\mathbf{A}$, looks at some input, $\mathbf{x}_t$, and outputs a value, $\mathbf{h}_t$. A loop in the network allows information to be passed from one step of the network to the next.

This diagram shows what a neural network looks like:

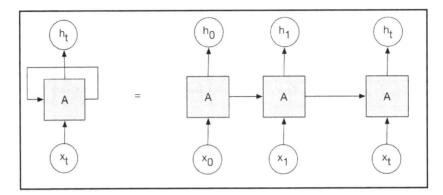

Simple RNNs for time series data

In this recipe, we will learn how to use a simple RNN implementation of Keras to predict sales based on a historical dataset.

RNNs are a class of artificial neural network where connections between nodes of the network form a directed graph along a sequence. This topology allows it to exhibit dynamic temporal behavior for input of the time sequence type. Unlike feedforward neural networks, RNNs can use their internal state (also called **memory**) to process sequences of inputs. This makes them suitable for tasks such as unsegmented, connected handwriting recognition or speech recognition.

A simple RNN is implemented as part of the `keras.layers.SimpleRNN` class as follows:

```
keras.layers.SimpleRNN(units, activation='tanh',
    use_bias=True,
    kernel_initializer='glorot_uniform',
    recurrent_initializer='orthogonal',
    bias_initializer='zeros',
    kernel_regularizer=None,
    recurrent_regularizer=None,
    bias_regularizer=None,
    activity_regularizer=None,
    kernel_constraint=None,
    recurrent_constraint=None,
    bias_constraint=None,
    dropout=0.0,
    recurrent_dropout=0.0,
```

```
    return_sequences=False,
    return_state=False,
    go_backwards=False,
    stateful=False,
    unroll=False)
```

A simple RNN is a fully-connected RNN where the output is to be fed back to the input. We will be using a simple RNN for time series prediction.

Getting ready

The dataset is in this file: `sales-of-shampoo-over-a-three-ye.csv`. It has two columns, the first for months and the second for sales figures for each month, as follows:

```
"Month","Sales of shampoo over a three year period"
"1-01",266.0
"1-02",145.9
"1-03",183.1
"1-04",119.3
"1-05",180.3
"1-06",168.5
"1-07",231.8
```

First, we need to import the relevant classes, as follows:

```
from pandas import read_csv
from matplotlib import pyplot
from pandas import datetime
```

Loading the dataset

1. We define a parser to convert YY to YYYY, shown as follow:

```
def parser(x):
    return datetime.strptime('200' + x, '%Y-%m')
```

2. Next, call the `read_csv` function of pandas to load a `.csv` file into a pandas DataFrame.

Notice the data parser being used is the function defined previously.

3. The next `read_csv` function is called in the next code:

```
series = read_csv('sales-of-shampoo-over-a-three-ye.csv', header=0,
parse_dates=[0], index_col=0,
                    squeeze=True, date_parser=parser)
```

4. Once the series is loaded, let's summarize the first few rows:

```
print(series.head())
```

The output of the preceding code is as follows:

```
Month
2001-01-01 266.0
2001-02-01 145.9
2001-03-01 183.1
2001-04-01 119.3
2001-05-01 180.3
```

5. Next, let's print the line plot using the `pyplot` library:

```
series.plot()
pyplot.show()
```

The next screenshot shows the line plot:

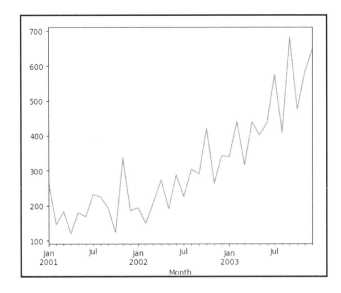

As can be seen, the sales are quite erratic but there is a trend line upwards.

How to do it...

1. Next, let's define the parameters to be used in our simple network, as well as the `DataFrame` where we are going to store the results, as follows:

```
n_lag = 1
n_repeats = 30
n_epochs = 1000
n_batch = 4
n_neurons = 3
results = DataFrame()
```

2. We then call the `experiment` method as follows:

```
results['results'] = experiment(series, n_lag, n_repeats, n_epochs,
n_batch, n_neurons)
```

Inside the `experiment()` method, we are processing the data through the network as follows:

```
def experiment(series, n_lag, n_repeats, n_epochs, n_batch,
n_neurons):
    # method details ....
```

3. First, we get values of the `series DataFrame`, as follows:

```
raw_values = series.values
diff_values = difference(raw_values, 1)
```

The output of `raw_values` and `diff values` is as follows:

```
raw_values :
[266. 145.9 183.1 119.3 180.3 168.5 231.8 224.5 192.8 122.9 336.5
185.9
 194.3 149.5 210.1 273.3 191.4 287. 226. 303.6 289.9 421.6 264.5
342.3
 339.7 440.4 315.9 439.3 401.3 437.4 575.5 407.6 682. 475.3 581.3
646.9]

diff values:

0 -120.1
1 37.2
2 -63.8
3 61.0
4 -11.8
5 63.3
```

```
6 -7.3
7 -31.7
8 -69.9
9 213.6
10 -150.6
...
```

The `diff values` are calculated by subtracting the next values from the previous ones, for example `145.9 - 266. = -120.1.`

4. Convert the time series to supervised values as follows:

```
supervised = timeseries_to_supervised(diff_values, n_lag)
```

Here, the `timeseries_to_supervised` method is as follows:

```
def timeseries_to_supervised(data, lag=1):
 df = DataFrame(data)
 columns = [df.shift(i) for i in range(1, lag + 1)]
 columns.append(df)
 df = concat(columns, axis=1)
 return df
```

The output of the supervised data frame is as follows:

```
0 0
 0 NaN -120.1
 1 -120.1 37.2
 2 37.2 -63.8
 3 -63.8 61.0
 4 61.0 -11.8
 5 -11.8 63.3
 6 63.3 -7.3
 7 -7.3 -31.7
 8 -31.7 -69.9
 9 -69.9 213.6
 10 213.6 -150.6
 11 -150.6 8.4
 12 8.4 -44.8
 13 -44.8 60.6
```

5. Next, we extract the `supervised_values` from the supervised data frame, as shown in the following code:

```
supervised_values = supervised.values[n_lag:, :]
```

The output of the preceding code is as follows:

```
[[-120.1 37.2]
 [ 37.2 -63.8]
 [ -63.8 61. ]
 [ 61. -11.8]
 [ -11.8 63.3]
 [ 63.3 -7.3]
 [ -7.3 -31.7]
 [ -31.7 -69.9]
 [ -69.9 213.6]
 [ 213.6 -150.6]
 [-150.6 8.4]
 [ 8.4 -44.8]
 [ -44.8 60.6]
 [ 60.6 63.2]
 [ 63.2 -81.9]
```

6. Split the supervised values into train and test data frames, as follows:

```
train, test = sup
ervised_values[0:-12], supervised_values[-12:]
```

The output of the train and test data frame is as follows:

```
train :
[[-120.1 37.2]
 [ 37.2 -63.8]
 [ -63.8 61. ]
 [ 61. -11.8]
 [ -11.8 63.3]
 [ 63.3 -7.3]
 [ -7.3 -31.7]
 [ -31.7 -69.9]
 [ -69.9 213.6]
 [ 213.6 -150.6]
 [-150.6 8.4]
 [ 8.4 -44.8]
 [ -44.8 60.6]
 [ 60.6 63.2]
 [ 63.2 -81.9]

test :
[[ 77.8 -2.6]
 [ -2.6 100.7]
 [ 100.7 -124.5]
 [-124.5 123.4]
 [ 123.4 -38. ]
```

```
[ -38.  36.1]
[ 36.1 138.1]
[ 138.1 -167.9]
[-167.9 274.4]
[ 274.4 -206.7]
[-206.7 106. ]
[ 106.  65.6]]
```

7. Next, we will normalize the train and test data frame, as follows:

```
scaler, train_scaled, test_scaled = scale(train, test)
```

The output of the `train_scaled` data frame is as follows:

```
train_scaled
[[-0.80037766 0.04828702]
 [ 0.04828702 -0.496628 ]
 [-0.496628 0.17669274]
 [ 0.17669274 -0.21607769]
 [-0.21607769 0.1891017 ]
 [ 0.1891017 -0.1917993 ]
 [-0.1917993 -0.32344214]
 [-0.32344214 -0.52953871]
 [-0.52953871 1. ]
 [ 1.
```

```
test_scaled
[[-0.80037766 0.04828702]
 [ 0.04828702 -0.496628 ]
 [-0.496628 0.17669274]
 [ 0.17669274 -0.21607769]
 [-0.21607769 0.1891017 ]
 [ 0.1891017 -0.1917993 ]
 [-0.1917993 -0.32344214]
 [-0.32344214 -0.52953871]
 [-0.52953871 1. ]
 [ 1.]
```

Now, we will run the scaled training dataset through the neural network and compute the weights, as follows:

1. We will train the model based on the number of repeats, `n_repeats`.
2. We get the training data frame trimmed to `train_scaled[2:, :]`. The `train_trimmed` data frame has the following output:

```
train_trimmed:
[[-0.496628 0.17669274]
```

```
[ 0.17669274 -0.21607769]
[-0.21607769 0.1891017 ]
[ 0.1891017 -0.1917993 ]
[-0.1917993 -0.32344214]
[-0.32344214 -0.52953871]
[-0.52953871 1. ]
[ 1. -0.96493121]
[-0.96493121 -0.10709469]
[-0.10709469
```

3. Next, we call `fit_rnn(train_trimmed, n_batch, n_epochs, n_neurons)`, which returns the `rnn` model. Let's look at the `fit_rnn` implementation, as follows:

```
def fit_rnn(train, n_batch, nb_epoch, n_neurons):
  X, y = train[:, 0:-1], train[:, -1]
  X = X.reshape(X.shape[0], 1, X.shape[1])
  model = Sequential()
  model.add(SimpleRNN(n_neurons, batch_input_shape=(n_batch,
X.shape[1], X.shape[2]),
     stateful=True))
  model.add(Dense(1))
  model.compile(loss='mean_squared_error', optimizer='adam')
  for i in range(nb_epoch):
      model.fit(X, y, epochs=1, batch_size=n_batch, verbose=0,
shuffle=False)
      model.reset_states()
return model
```

First, we get `X`, `y` from `train_trimmed`. The values of `X` and `y` are:

```
X :
 [[-0.496628 ]
 [ 0.17669274]
 [-0.21607769]
 [ 0.1891017 ]
 [-0.1917993 ]
 [-0.32344214]
 [-0.52953871]
 [ 1. ]
 [-0.96493121]
 [-0.10709469]
 [-0.39411923]
 [ 0.17453466]
 [ 0.18856218]
 [-0.59428109]
 [ 0.3633666 ]
 [-0.48152145]
```

```
[ 0.26625303]

y :
 [ 0.17669274 -0.21607769 0.1891017 -0.1917993 -0.32344214
-0.52953871
 1. -0.96493121 -0.10709469 -0.39411923 0.17453466 0.18856218
 -0.59428109 0.3633666 -0.48152145 0.26625303 -0.22632857
0.55813326
 -1. 0.26733207]
```

Instantiate a sequential model

Next, we instantiate a sequential model and add the following layers:

- A simple RNN
- A dense layer with one output

Following are the steps of a simple RNN:

1. The next code listing shows model creation and compilation:

```
model = Sequential()
 model.add(SimpleRNN(n_neurons, batch_input_shape=(n_batch,
X.shape[1], X.shape[2]),
 stateful=True))
 model.add(Dense(1))
```

2. Then, we compile the model using `model. compile(..)` with loss and optimizers, shown as follows:

```
model.compile(loss='mean_squared_error', optimizer='adam')
```

We are using **mean squared error** (**MSE**) as the loss function and Adam as an optimizer. MSE is a loss function that uses a sum of squared difference between the predicted value and actual value divided by *1/n*, where *n* is the total sample

$$MSE = \frac{1}{n}\sum_{i=0}^{i=n}(Y_i - \hat{Y}_i)^2$$

size   .

Adaptive Moment Estimation (**Adam**) is another optimization method that computes adjustable learning rates for each of the parameters. It stores an exponentially decaying average of previous squared gradients, v_t. Adam also keeps an exponentially decaying average of past gradients, mt, like momentum. Momentum can be seen as a ball running down a slope. Adam behaves like a heavy ball with friction, which thus prefers flat minima in the error surface. We compute the decaying averages of past and past squared gradients m_t and v_t, respectively, as follows:

$$m_t = \beta_1 m_{t-1} + (1 - \beta_1)g_t$$
$$v_t = \beta_2 v_{t-1} + (1 - \beta_2)g_t^2$$

Since m_t and v_t are initialized as vectors of 0, they are biased towards 0s when decay rates β_1 and β_2 are 1. Hence, we calculate bias adjusted values $\hat{m}_t$ and $\hat{v}_t$:

$$\widehat{m_t} = \frac{m_t}{1 - \beta^t_1}$$

$$\widehat{v_t} = \frac{v_t}{1 - \beta^t_2}$$

The updated rule for Θ is shown as follows:

$$\theta_{t+1} = \theta_t - \frac{\eta}{\sqrt{v_t} + \epsilon}\hat{m}_t$$

Adam is implemented by Keras using the following function:

```
keras.optimizers.Adam(lr=0.001, beta_1=0.9, beta_2=0.999,
epsilon=None, decay=0.0, amsgrad=False)
```

3. Next, we update the model parameters by running the training data through it, as follows:

```
for i in range(nb_epoch):
    model.fit(X, y, epochs=1, batch_size=n_batch, verbose=0,
shuffle=False)
    model.reset_states()
```

4. Finally, we return the model, as follows:

```
return model
```

Next, we implement the following steps:

1. Reshape the test data `test_reshaped` and run it through the model to find predictions
2. Call `rnn_model.predict(....)`
3. Find `yhat` with `invert_scale` and `inverse_difference`
4. Store predictions in the `predictions` list
5. Calculate the RMSE
6. Print the RMSE for each iteration:

```
test_reshaped = test_scaled[:, 0:-1]
test_reshaped = test_reshaped.reshape(len(test_reshaped), 1, 1)
output = rnn_model.predict(test_reshaped, batch_size=n_batch)
predictions = list()
for i in range(len(output)):
  yhat = output[i, 0]
  X = test_scaled[i, 0:-1]
  # invert scaling
  yhat = invert_scale(scaler, X, yhat)
  # invert differencing
  yhat = inverse_difference(raw_values, yhat, len(test_scaled) + 1
- i)
  # store forecast
  predictions.append(yhat)
# report performance
rmse = sqrt(mean_squared_error(raw_values[-12:], predictions))
print('%d) Test RMSE: %.3f' % (r + 1, rmse))
error_scores.append(rmse)
```

7. The complete code listing for model creation and `error_scores` calculation is as follows:

```
error_scores = list()
for r in range(n_repeats):
  # fit the model
  train_trimmed = train_scaled[2:, :]
  rnn_model = fit_rnn(train_trimmed, n_batch, n_epochs, n_neurons)
  # forecast test dataset
  test_reshaped = test_scaled[:, 0:-1]
  test_reshaped = test_reshaped.reshape(len(test_reshaped), 1, 1)
  output = lstm_model.predict(test_reshaped, batch_size=n_batch)
  predictions = list()
  for i in range(len(output)):
    yhat = output[i, 0]
    X = test_scaled[i, 0:-1]
    # invert scaling
```

```
yhat = invert_scale(scaler, X, yhat)
# invert differencing
yhat = inverse_difference(raw_values, yhat, len(test_scaled) +
1 - i)
# store forecast
predictions.append(yhat)
# report performance
rmse = sqrt(mean_squared_error(raw_values[-12:], predictions))
print('%d) Test RMSE: %.3f' % (r + 1, rmse))
error_scores.append(rmse)
```

8. The RMSE scores obtained for 30 iterations are as follows:

```
1) Test RMSE: 95.838
2) Test RMSE: 75.151
3) Test RMSE: 98.616
4) Test RMSE: 108.205
5) Test RMSE: 83.807
6) Test RMSE: 73.411
...
25) Test RMSE: 86.076
26) Test RMSE: 86.104
27) Test RMSE: 85.667
28) Test RMSE: 74.321
29) Test RMSE: 88.347
30) Test RMSE: 97.868
```

9. A summary of the RMSE iteration and plot is as follows:

```
      results
count 30.000000
mean 86.546032
std 9.338947
min 71.019965
25% 81.406349
50% 85.000358
75% 92.118326
max 108.008031
```

The screenshot of the RMSE iteration and plot is as follows:

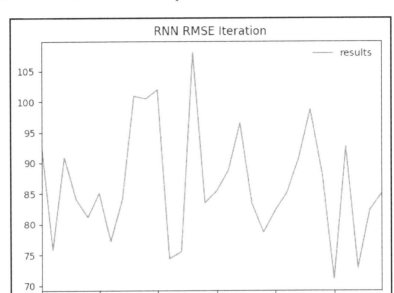

As can be seen from the preceding plot, the RMSE varies between 73 and 108 over the iterations, but becomes a little more stable with time.

LSTM networks for time series data

In this recipe, we will learn what LSTM networks are and how can they be leveraged to better predict time series data with long-term memory characteristics.

LSTM networks

LSTM is designed to avoid the long-term dependency problem. It remembers the information for a longer period of time.

All recurrent neural networks have the form of a chain of repeating modules of a neural network. In standard RNNs, this repeating module will have a very simple structure, such as a single tanh layer. LSTMs also have this chain-like structure, but the repeating module has a different structure.

There are four layers, interacting in a very special way, as shown in the following diagram:

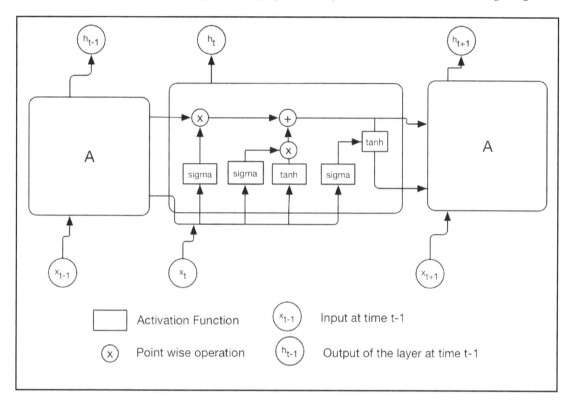

Reference: http://colah.github.io/posts/2015-08-Understanding-LSTMs/

We will not go into more detail on how an LSTM works, but focus on how it is used in Keras.

LSTM memory example

In this recipe, we will learn, with a simple example, how an LSTM network remembers the value in a step from the distant past. We will input two sequences and the LSTM will remember which character to output based on the first sequence input, as follows:

```
seq1 = ['A', 'B', 'C', 'D', 'A']
seq2 = ['Z', 'B', 'C', 'D', 'Z']
```

Getting ready

Import the relevant Python packages and classes from `pandas`, `numpy`, and `keras`:

```
from pandas import DataFrame
import numpy as np
np.random.seed(1337)
from keras.models import Sequential
from keras.layers import Dense
from keras.layers import LSTM
```

How to do it...

Let us get into the implementation on how to make an LSTM model predict the next character while remembering the sequence beyond the immediate past.

Encoder

1. First, we define an encoder, which converts `char` to a one-hot encoded value in an array of length 91:

```
def encode(pattern, n_unique):
    encoded = list()
    for value in pattern:
        row = [0.0 for x in range(n_unique)]
        index = ord(value)
        row[ord(value)] = 1.0
        encoded.append(row)
    return encoded
```

2. Divide the sequence into x and y values as follows:

```
def to_xy_pairs(encoded):
    X,y = list(),list()
    for i in range(1, len(encoded)):
        X.append(encoded[i-1])
        y.append(encoded[i])
    return X, y
```

3. Convert the x, y values into a three-dimensional matrix which LSTM can understand, as follows:

```
def to_lstm_dataset(sequence, n_unique):
    # one hot encode
    encoded = encode(sequence, n_unique)
    # convert to in/out patterns
    X,y = to_xy_pairs(encoded)
    # convert to LSTM friendly format
    dfX, dfy = DataFrame(X), DataFrame(y)
    lstmX = dfX.values
    lstmX = lstmX.reshape(lstmX.shape[0], 1, lstmX.shape[1])
    lstmY = dfy.values
    return lstmX, lstmY
```

4. Notice how a pandas DataFrame is created from X, y, and lstmX (dfX.values) is reshaped to input to model.fit:

```
seq1 = ['A', 'B', 'C', 'D', 'A']
seq2 = ['Z', 'B', 'C', 'D', 'Z']
print(ord('z'))
# convert sequences into required data format
#n_unique = len(set(seq1 + seq2))
n_unique = ord('Z') +1
seq1X, seq1Y = to_lstm_dataset(seq1, n_unique)
seq2X, seq2Y = to_lstm_dataset(seq2, n_unique)
```

LSTM configuration and model

1. We define the LSTM configuration; we come up with the values empirically to get the desired output, as follows:

```
# define LSTM configuration
n_neurons = 200
n_batch = 1
n_epoch = 1000
n_features = n_unique
```

2. Now, we define the actual model, using LSTM as one of the layers, as follows:

```
model = Sequential()
model.add(LSTM(n_neurons, batch_input_shape=(n_batch, 1,
n_features), stateful=True))
model.add(Dense(n_unique, activation='sigmoid'))
model.compile(loss='binary_crossentropy', optimizer='adam')
```

Notice that we are using a two-layer network with LSTM as one layer followed by a dense layer. The activation function being used is `sigmoid` and the loss function being used is `binary_crossentropy`.

3. The cross-entropy measure can be used as an alternative to squared error. Cross-entropy is used as an error measure when a network's outputs represent independent hypotheses (for example, each node stands for a different concept). The node activations can be understood as representing the probability (or confidence) that each hypothesis might be true. The output vector represents a probability distribution, and error measure-cross-entropy is the distance between what the network believes this distribution should be and what it should be.

4. Cross-entropy is more useful in problems in which the targets are 0 and 1 (though the outputs obviously may assume values in between). Cross-entropy tends to allow errors to change weights even when nodes saturate (which means that their derivatives are asymptotically close to 0).

5. We are using Adam as an optimization technique for gradient descent next:

Adam is another optimization method which computes adjustable learning rates for each of the parameters. It stores an exponentially decaying average of previous squared gradients v_t. Adam also keeps an exponentially decaying average of past gradients mt, like momentum. Momentum can be seen as a ball running down a slope; Adam behaves like a heavy ball with friction, which thus prefers flat minima in the error surface. We compute the decaying averages of past and past squared gradients m_t and v_t respectively as follows:

$$m_t = \beta_1 m_{t-1} + (1 - \beta_1)g_t$$
$$v_t = \beta_2 v_{t-1} + (1 - \beta_2)g_t^2$$

Since m_t and v_t are initialized as vectors of 0, they are biased towards 0s when decay rates β_1 and β_2 are 1. Hence, we calculate the bias adjusted values $\widehat{m}_t$ and $\hat{v}_t$ as follows:

$$\widehat{m_t} = \frac{m_t}{1 - \beta^t{}_1}$$

$$\widehat{v_t} = \frac{v_t}{1 - \beta^t{}_2}$$

The updated rule for Θ is shown as follows:

$$\theta_{t+1} = \theta_t - \frac{\eta}{\sqrt{v_t} + \epsilon} \hat{m}_t$$

Adam is implemented by Keras using the following function:

```
keras.optimizers.Adam(lr=0.001, beta_1=0.9, beta_2=0.999,
epsilon=None, decay=0.0, amsgrad=False)
```

Train the model

1. Once the network is compiled, it is trained on the test data as follows:

```
# train LSTM
for i in range(n_epoch):
model.fit(seq1X, seq1Y, epochs=1, batch_size=n_batch, verbose=1,
shuffle=False)
model.reset_states()
model.fit(seq2X, seq2Y, epochs=1, batch_size=n_batch, verbose=0,
shuffle=False)
model.reset_states()
```

2. The last step is to test against sequences one and two, shown as follows:

```
# test LSTM on sequence 1
print('Sequence 1')
result = model.predict_classes(seq1X, batch_size=n_batch,
verbose=0)
model.reset_states()
for i in range(len(result)):
    print('X=%s y=%s, yhat=%s' % (seq1[i], seq1[i+1],
chr(result[i])))

# test LSTM on sequence 2
print('Sequence 2')
result = model.predict_classes(seq2X, batch_size=n_batch,
verbose=0)
model.reset_states()
for i in range(len(result)):
    print('X=%s y=%s, yhat=%s' % (seq2[i], seq2[i+1],
chr(result[i])))
```

3. The output from the tests conducted demonstrates long-term memory capabilities, shown as follows:

```
Sequence 1
  X=A  y=B,  yhat=B
  X=B  y=C,  yhat=C
  X=C  y=D,  yhat=D
  X=D  y=A,  yhat=A
  Sequence 2
  X=Z  y=B,  yhat=B
  X=B  y=C,  yhat=C
  X=C  y=D,  yhat=D
  X=D  y=Z,  yhat=Z
```

The code listing that follows shows the complete logic.

Full code listing

The full code listing code is as follows:

```
from pandas import DataFrame
import numpy as np
np.random.seed(1337)
from keras.models import Sequential
from keras.layers import Dense
from keras.layers import LSTM

# binary encode an input pattern, by converting characters into int
# return a list of binary vectors
def encode(pattern, n_unique):
    encoded = list()
    for value in pattern:
        row = [0.0 for x in range(n_unique)]
        index = ord(value)
        row[ord(value)] = 1.0
        encoded.append(row)
    return encoded


# create input/output pairs of encoded vectors, returns X, y
def to_xy_pairs(encoded):
    X,y = list(),list()
    for i in range(1, len(encoded)):
        X.append(encoded[i-1])
        y.append(encoded[i])
    return X, y
```

```python
# convert sequence to x/y pairs ready for use with an LSTM
def to_lstm_dataset(sequence, n_unique):
    # one hot encode
    encoded = encode(sequence, n_unique)
    # convert to in/out patterns
    X,y = to_xy_pairs(encoded)
    # convert to LSTM friendly format
    dfX, dfy = DataFrame(X), DataFrame(y)
    lstmX = dfX.values
    lstmX = lstmX.reshape(lstmX.shape[0], 1, lstmX.shape[1])
    lstmY = dfy.values
    return lstmX, lstmY


seq1 = ['A', 'B', 'C', 'D', 'A']
seq2 = ['Z', 'B', 'C', 'D', 'Z']
print(ord('z'))
# convert sequences into required data format
#n_unique = len(set(seq1 + seq2))
n_unique = ord('Z') +1
seq1X, seq1Y = to_lstm_dataset(seq1, n_unique)
seq2X, seq2Y = to_lstm_dataset(seq2, n_unique)
# define LSTM configuration
n_neurons = 200
n_batch = 1
n_epoch = 1000
n_features = n_unique
# create LSTM
model = Sequential()
model.add(LSTM(n_neurons, batch_input_shape=(n_batch, 1, n_features),
stateful=True))
model.add(Dense(n_unique, activation='sigmoid'))
model.compile(loss='binary_crossentropy', optimizer='adam')
# train LSTM
for i in range(n_epoch):
    model.fit(seq1X, seq1Y, epochs=1, batch_size=n_batch, verbose=1,
shuffle=False)
    model.reset_states()
    model.fit(seq2X, seq2Y, epochs=1, batch_size=n_batch, verbose=0,
shuffle=False)
    model.reset_states()

# test LSTM on sequence 1
print('Sequence 1')
result = model.predict_classes(seq1X, batch_size=n_batch, verbose=0)
model.reset_states()
for i in range(len(result)):
    print('X=%s y=%s, yhat=%s' % (seq1[i], seq1[i+1], chr(result[i])))
```

```
# test LSTM on sequence 2
print('Sequence 2')
result = model.predict_classes(seq2X, batch_size=n_batch, verbose=0)
model.reset_states()
for i in range(len(result)):
    print('X=%s y=%s, yhat=%s' % (seq2[i], seq2[i+1], chr(result[i])))
```

Time series forecasting with LSTM

In this recipe, we will learn how to use the LSTM implementation of Keras to predict sales based on a historical dataset. We will use the same dataset we used earlier for predicting shampoo sales.

Getting ready

The dataset is in the `sales-of-shampoo-over-a-three-ye.csv` file:

```
"Month","Sales of shampoo over a three year period"
"1-01",266.0
"1-02",145.9
"1-03",183.1
"1-04",119.3
"1-05",180.3
"1-06",168.5
"1-07",231.8
```

First, we need to import the relevant classes as follows:

```
from pandas import read_csv
from matplotlib import pyplot
from pandas import datetime
```

Load the dataset

1. First, we define a parser to convert YY to YYYY:

```
def parser(x):
    return datetime.strptime('200' + x, '%Y-%m')
```

2. Next, call the `read_csv` function of pandas to load a `.csv` into a `DataFrame` as follows:

```
series = read_csv('sales-of-shampoo-over-a-three-ye.csv', header=0,
parse_dates=[0], index_col=0, squeeze=True,
date_parser=parser)
```

3. Summarize the first few rows using the following code:

```
print(series.head())
```

The output of the preceding code is as follows:

```
Month
2001-01-01  266.0
2001-02-01  145.9
2001-03-01  183.1
2001-04-01  119.3
2001-05-01  180.3
```

4. Let's print the line plot using the following code:

```
series.plot()
pyplot.show()
```

The output of the line plot is as follows:

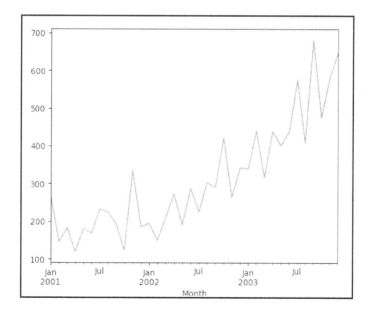

How to do it...

1. Next, let's define the parameters to be used in our LSTM network, as well as the `DataFrame` where we are going to store the results:

```
n_lag = 1
n_repeats = 30
n_epochs = 1000
n_batch = 4
n_neurons = 3
results = DataFrame()
```

2. We then call the `experiment` method as follows:

```
results['results'] = experiment(series, n_lag, n_repeats, n_epochs,
n_batch, n_neurons)
```

Inside the `experiment()` method, we process the data through the network as follows:

```
def experiment(series, n_lag, n_repeats, n_epochs, n_batch,
n_neurons):
  # method details ....
```

3. First, we get the values of the `series` data frame as follows:

```
raw_values = series.values
diff_values = difference(raw_values, 1)
```

The output of the values of the `series` data frame is as follows:

```
raw_values :
[266. 145.9 183.1 119.3 180.3 168.5 231.8 224.5 192.8 122.9 336.5
185.9
 194.3 149.5 210.1 273.3 191.4 287. 226. 303.6 289.9 421.6 264.5
342.3
 339.7 440.4 315.9 439.3 401.3 437.4 575.5 407.6 682. 475.3 581.3
646.9]
diff values:
 0 -120.1
 1 37.2
 2 -63.8
 3 61.0
 4 -11.8
 5 63.3
 6 -7.3
 7 -31.7
```

```
8 -69.9
9 213.6
10 -150.6
. . .
```

Different values are calculated by subtracting the following values from the previous, for example, `145.9 - 266. = -120.1`.

4. Convert the time series to supervised values, as follows:

```
supervised = timeseries_to_supervised(diff_values, n_lag)
```

5. Here, the `timeseries_to_supervised` method is as follows:

```
def timeseries_to_supervised(data, lag=1):
 df = DataFrame(data)
 columns = [df.shift(i) for i in range(1, lag + 1)]
 columns.append(df)
 df = concat(columns, axis=1)
 return df
```

The output of the supervised `DataFrame` is listed as follows:

```
0  0
0  NaN -120.1
1  -120.1 37.2
2  37.2 -63.8
3  -63.8 61.0
4  61.0 -11.8
5  -11.8 63.3
6  63.3 -7.3
7  -7.3 -31.7
8  -31.7 -69.9
9  -69.9 213.6
10 213.6 -150.6
11 -150.6 8.4
12 8.4 -44.8
13 -44.8 60.6
```

6. Next, we extract the `supervised_values` from the supervised data frame, as shown in the following code:

```
supervised_values = supervised.values[n_lag:, :]
```

The output of the supervised values from the supervised data frame is listed as follows:

```
[[-120.1 37.2]
 [ 37.2 -63.8]
 [ -63.8 61. ]
 [ 61. -11.8]
 [ -11.8 63.3]
 [ 63.3 -7.3]
 [ -7.3 -31.7]
 [ -31.7 -69.9]
 [ -69.9 213.6]
 [ 213.6 -150.6]
 [-150.6 8.4]
 [ 8.4 -44.8]
 [ -44.8 60.6]
 [ 60.6 63.2]
 [ 63.2 -81.9]
```

7. Split the supervised values to train and test data frame, as follows:

```
train, test = supervised_values[0:-12], supervised_values[-12:]
```

The output of the supervised values for the train and test data frame is listed as follows:

```
train :
[[-120.1 37.2]
 [ 37.2 -63.8]
 [ -63.8 61. ]
 [ 61. -11.8]
 [ -11.8 63.3]
 [ 63.3 -7.3]
 [ -7.3 -31.7]
 [ -31.7 -69.9]
 [ -69.9 213.6]
 [ 213.6 -150.6]
 [-150.6 8.4]
 [ 8.4 -44.8]
 [ -44.8 60.6]
 [ 60.6 63.2]
 [ 63.2 -81.9]

test :

[[ 77.8 -2.6]
 [ -2.6 100.7]
 [ 100.7 -124.5]
```

```
[-124.5 123.4]
[ 123.4 -38. ]
[ -38. 36.1]
[ 36.1 138.1]
[ 138.1 -167.9]
[-167.9 274.4]
[ 274.4 -206.7]
[-206.7 106. ]
[ 106. 65.6]]
```

8. Next, we will normalize the train and test data frame, as follows:

```
scaler, train_scaled, test_scaled = scale(train, test)
```

The output of the train and test data frame is as follows:

```
train_scaled
[[-0.80037766 0.04828702]
 [ 0.04828702 -0.496628 ]
 [-0.496628 0.17669274]
 [ 0.17669274 -0.21607769]
 [-0.21607769 0.1891017 ]
 [ 0.1891017 -0.1917993 ]
 [-0.1917993 -0.32344214]
 [-0.32344214 -0.52953871]
 [-0.52953871 1. ]
 [ 1.
test_scaled
[[-0.80037766 0.04828702]
 [ 0.04828702 -0.496628 ]
 [-0.496628 0.17669274]
 [ 0.17669274 -0.21607769]
 [-0.21607769 0.1891017 ]
 [ 0.1891017 -0.1917993 ]
 [-0.1917993 -0.32344214]
 [-0.32344214 -0.52953871]
 [-0.52953871 1. ]
 [ 1.]
```

Now, we will run the scaled training dataset through the neural network and compute the weights, as follows:

1. We will train the model based on number of repeats, `n_repeats`

2. We get the training data frame trimmed with `train_scaled[2:, :]train_trimmed` has the following output:

```
train_trimmed:
[[-0.496628 0.17669274]
```

```
[ 0.17669274 -0.21607769]
[-0.21607769 0.1891017 ]
[ 0.1891017 -0.1917993 ]
[-0.1917993 -0.32344214]
[-0.32344214 -0.52953871]
[-0.52953871 1. ]
[ 1. -0.96493121]
[-0.96493121 -0.10709469]
[-0.10709469
```

3. Next, we call `fit_lstm(train_trimmed, n_batch, n_epochs, n_neurons)`, which returns `lstm_model`.

   Let's look at the `fit_lstm` implementation as follows:

```
def fit_lstm(train, n_batch, nb_epoch, n_neurons):
    X, y = train[:, 0:-1], train[:, -1]
    X = X.reshape(X.shape[0], 1, X.shape[1])
    model = Sequential()
    model.add(LSTM(n_neurons, batch_input_shape=(n_batch, X.shape[1],
X.shape[2]),
        stateful=True))
    model.add(Dense(1))
    model.compile(loss='mean_squared_error', optimizer='adam')
    for i in range(nb_epoch):
        model.fit(X, y, epochs=1, batch_size=n_batch, verbose=0,
shuffle=False)
        model.reset_states()
return model
```

4. First, we get `X`, `y` from `train_trimmed`. The values of `X` and `y` are as follows:

```
X :
 [[-0.496628 ]
 [ 0.17669274]
 [-0.21607769]
 [ 0.1891017 ]
 [-0.1917993 ]
 [-0.32344214]
 [-0.52953871]
 [ 1. ]
 [-0.96493121]
 [-0.10709469]
 [-0.39411923]
 [ 0.17453466]
 [ 0.18856218]
 [-0.59428109]
 [ 0.3633666 ]
```

```
      [-0.48152145]
      [ 0.26625303]
   y :
      [ 0.17669274 -0.21607769 0.1891017 -0.1917993 -0.32344214
   -0.52953871
      1. -0.96493121 -0.10709469 -0.39411923 0.17453466 0.18856218
      -0.59428109 0.3633666 -0.48152145 0.26625303 -0.22632857
   0.55813326
      -1. 0.26733207]
```

Instantiate a sequential model

Here we instantiate a sequential model and add the following layers:

- LSTM
- Dense

The following steps describe the preceding points in detail:

1. The dense layer with one output is as follows:

   ```
   model = Sequential()
    model.add(LSTM(n_neurons, batch_input_shape=(n_batch, X.shape[1],
   X.shape[2]),
    stateful=True))
    model.add(Dense(1))
   ```

2. Then, we compile the model using model. compile(..), with loss and optimizers, shown as follows:

   ```
   model.compile(loss='mean_squared_error', optimizer='adam')
   ```

3. We are using MSE as the loss function and Adam as an optimizer. MSE is a loss function that uses a sum of squared difference between the predicted value and the actual value divided by *1/n* where *n* is the total sample size.

$$MSE = \frac{1}{n}\sum_{i=0}^{i=n}(Y_i - \hat{Y}_i)^2$$

Adaptive Moment Estimation (**Adam**) is another optimization method which computes adjustable learning rates for each of the parameter. It stores an exponentially decaying average of previous squared gradients v_t. Adam also keeps an exponentially decaying average of past gradients mt, like momentum. Momentum can be seen as a ball running down a slope. Adam behaves like a heavy ball with friction, which thus prefers flat minima in the error surface. We compute the decaying averages of past and past squared gradients m_t and v_t respectively as follows:

$$m_t = \beta_1 m_{t-1} + (1 - \beta_1) g_t$$
$$v_t = \beta_2 v_{t-1} + (1 - \beta_2) g_t^2$$

Since m_t and v_t are initialized as vectors of 0, they are biased towards 0s when decay rates β_1 and β_2 are 1. Hence, we calculate the bias adjusted values $\hat{m}_t$ and $\hat{v}_t$ as follows:

$$\widehat{m_t} = \frac{m_t}{1 - \beta^t{}_1}$$

$$\widehat{v_t} = \frac{v_t}{1 - \beta^t{}_2}$$

The updated rule for Θ is shown as follows:

$$\theta_{t+1} = \theta_t - \frac{\eta}{\sqrt{v_t} + \in} \hat{m}_t$$

4. Adam is implemented by Keras using the following function:

```
keras.optimizers.Adam(lr=0.001, beta_1=0.9, beta_2=0.999,
epsilon=None, decay=0.0, amsgrad=False)
```

5. Next, we update the model parameters by running the training data through it, as follows:

```
for i in range(nb_epoch):
    model.fit(X, y, epochs=1, batch_size=n_batch, verbose=0,
shuffle=False)
    model.reset_states()
```

6. Finally, we return the model, as follows:

```
return model
```

Next, we implement the following steps:

1. Reshape the `test_reshaped` test data and run it through the model to find predictions
2. Call `lstm_model.predict`
3. Find `yhat` with `invert_scale` and `inverse_difference`
4. Store predictions in the `predictions` list
5. Calculate the RMSE
6. Print the RMSE for each iteration

The code is as follows:

1. Starting from reshaping `test_reshaped`:

```
test_reshaped = test_scaled[:, 0:-1]
 test_reshaped = test_reshaped.reshape(len(test_reshaped), 1, 1)
 output = lstm_model.predict(test_reshaped, batch_size=n_batch)
 predictions = list()
 for i in range(len(output)):
   yhat = output[i, 0]
   X = test_scaled[i, 0:-1]
   # invert scaling
   yhat = invert_scale(scaler, X, yhat)
   # invert differencing
   yhat = inverse_difference(raw_values, yhat, len(test_scaled) + 1
 - i)
   # store forecast
   predictions.append(yhat)
 # report performance
 rmse = sqrt(mean_squared_error(raw_values[-12:], predictions))
 print('%d) Test RMSE: %.3f' % (r + 1, rmse))
 error_scores.append(rmse)
```

2. The complete code listing for model creation and `error_scores` calculation is as follows:

```
error_scores = list()
for r in range(n_repeats):
  # fit the model
  train_trimmed = train_scaled[2:, :]
  lstm_model = fit_lstm(train_trimmed, n_batch, n_epochs,
n_neurons)
  # forecast test dataset
  test_reshaped = test_scaled[:, 0:-1]
```

```
test_reshaped = test_reshaped.reshape(len(test_reshaped), 1, 1)
output = lstm_model.predict(test_reshaped, batch_size=n_batch)
predictions = list()
for i in range(len(output)):
  yhat = output[i, 0]
  X = test_scaled[i, 0:-1]
  # invert scaling
  yhat = invert_scale(scaler, X, yhat)
  # invert differencing
  yhat = inverse_difference(raw_values, yhat, len(test_scaled) +
1 - i)
  # store forecast
  predictions.append(yhat)
 # report performance
 rmse = sqrt(mean_squared_error(raw_values[-12:], predictions))
 print('%d) Test RMSE: %.3f' % (r + 1, rmse))
 error_scores.append(rmse)
```

3. The RMSE scores obtained are as follows:

```
RMSE
 1) Test RMSE: 99.392
 2) Test RMSE: 91.873
 3) Test RMSE: 101.440
 4) Test RMSE: 89.926
 5) Test RMSE: 90.300
 6) Test RMSE: 101.218
 7) Test RMSE: 93.807
 8) Test RMSE: 94.887
 9) Test RMSE: 95.090
 10) Test RMSE: 92.210
 11) Test RMSE: 98.373
 12) Test RMSE: 96.900
 13) Test RMSE: 99.465
 14) Test RMSE: 91.884
```

4. A summary of the RMSE scores plotted against iterations is as follows:

```
results
 count 30.000000
 mean 96.420240
 std 5.120269
 min 88.793766
 25% 92.659372
 50% 95.393612
 75% 99.786859
 max 107.698912
```

The screenshot of the preceding code is as follows:

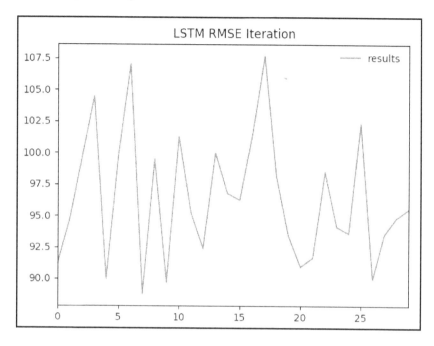

Observation

Notice that the RMSE variation is lower than the simple RNN but the mean is higher for the LSTM (96.42) than for the simple RNN (86.54).

Sequence to sequence learning for the same length output with LSTM

In this recipe, we will learn how to use LSTM to predict a value that is of the same or a slightly different length, such as subtraction of two numbers.

Getting ready

Create a `requirements.txt` with Keras and `six.moves` dependencies. Import the relevant classes from `keras`, `numpy`, and `six.moves` as follows:

```
from __future__ import print_function
from keras.models import Sequential
from keras import layers
import numpy as np
import six.moves
```

In the next section, we will learn how to implement an LSTM network that can handle any three-digit subtraction.

How to do it...

1. Create a character table that can handle encoding and decoding. This class has three methods, as follows:
   - `__init__()`
   - `encode()`
   - `decode()`

2. The code is as follows:

```
class CharTable(object):
    def __init__(self, char):
        self.char = sorted(set(char))
        self.char_indices = dict((ch, i) for i, ch in
enumerate(self.char))
        self.indices_char = dict((i, ch) for i, ch in
enumerate(self.char))

    def encode(self, C, num_rows):
        x = np.zeros((num_rows, len(self.char)))
        for i, ch in enumerate(C):
            x[i, self.char_indices[ch]] = 1
        return x
    def decode(self, x, calc_argmax=True):
        if calc_argmax:
            x = x.argmax(axis=-1)
        return ''.join(self.indices_char[x] for x in x)
```

3. Next, we define some utility constants to be used to display the final test results as well as the training data size, count of digits of numbers we want to subtract from each other, and whether we want to train reverse examples as well. Reverse the query, example, `12-345` becomes `543-21`:

```
lass colors:
    ok = '\033[92m'
    fail = '\033[91m'
    close = '\033[0m'

# Parameters for the model and dataset.
TRAINING_SIZE = 50000
DIGITS = 3
REVERSE = True
```

4. Maximum length of the input, which in this case is `3 + 3 +1 = 7`, for example `300-200 = 7` digits . 300 is 3 digits, - is one digit and 200 is 3 digits, hence the total is 7 digits. The code is as follows:

```
MAXLEN = DIGITS + 1 + DIGITS
```

5. Next, we define the characters and the instance of the character table, as follows:

```
chars = '0123456789- '
ctable = CharTable(chars)
```

Training data

1. Next, we generate the training data by generating two random three-digit numbers (which is x in this case), subtracting them, and generating y as follows:

```
questions = []
expected = []
seen = set()
print('Generating data...')
while len(questions) < TRAINING_SIZE:
    f = lambda: int(''.join(np.random.choice(list('0123456789'))
                    for i in range(np.random.randint(1, DIGITS +
1)))))
    a, b = f(), f()
    # Skip any subtraction questions we've already seen
    # Also skip any such that x-Y == Y-x (hence the sorting).
    key = tuple(sorted((a, b)))
    if key in seen:
        continue
```

```
        seen.add(key)
        # Pad the data with spaces such that it is always MAXLEN.
        q = '{}-{}'.format(a, b)
        query = q + ' ' * (MAXLEN - len(q))
        ans = str(a - b)
        # Answers can be of maximum size DIGITS + 1.
        ans += ' ' * (DIGITS + 1 - len(ans))
        if REVERSE:
            # Reverse the query, e.g., '12-345 ' becomes ' 543-21'.
(Note the
            # space used for padding.)
            query = query[::-1]
        questions.append(query)
        expected.append(ans)
    print('Total subtraction questions:', len(questions))
```

2. Once the training data is generated, we vectorize it using the character table as follows:

```
print('Vectorization:')
x = np.zeros((len(questions), MAXLEN, len(chars)), dtype=np.bool)
y = np.zeros((len(questions), DIGITS + 1, len(chars)),
dtype=np.bool)
for i, sentence in enumerate(questions):
 x[i] = ctable.encode(sentence, MAXLEN)
for i, sentence in enumerate(expected):
 y[i] = ctable.encode(sentence, DIGITS + 1)
```

3. Next, we shuffle the values of x and y as follows:

```
indices = np.arange(len(y))
np.random.shuffle(indices)
x = x[indices]
y = y[indices]
```

4. We need to set 10% for validation data, which we never train over. Find the value of the index where the split needs to happen, 45000 in this case:

```
split_at = len(x) - len(x) // 10
(x_train, x_val) = x[:split_at], x[split_at:]
(y_train, y_val) = y[:split_at], y[split_at:]
```

5. Print the shape of the training and validation data as follows:

```
Training Data:
(45000, 7, 12)
(45000, 4, 12)
Validation Data:
(5000, 7, 12)
```

Model creation

1. Define the hyperparameters of the model:

```
RNN = layers.LSTM
HIDDEN_SIZE = 128
BATCH_SIZE = 128
LAYERS = 1
```

2. Next, we define the sequential model and add various layers to it, as follows:

```
print('Build model:')
model = Sequential()
# "Encode" the input sequence using an RNN, producing an output of
HIDDEN_SIZE.
# Note: For situation where input sequences have a variable length,
# use input_shape=(None, num_feature).
model.add(RNN(HIDDEN_SIZE, input_shape=(MAXLEN, len(chars))))
model.add(layers.RepeatVector(DIGITS + 1))
for _ in range(LAYERS):
 model.add(RNN(HIDDEN_SIZE, return_sequences=True))
model.add(layers.TimeDistributed(layers.Dense(len(chars))))
model.add(layers.Activation('softmax'))
```

3. An input to the first LSTM layer of input `HIDDEN_SIZE` (128 in this case) is a shape with the following parameters:
   - Number of time steps (`MAXLEN`)
   - Number of features (`len(chars)` in the previous sample)

It uses the repeat vector layer to get the input, which is repeated `DIGITS+1` times.

Another LSTM layer is added, which returns the hidden state update the number of time steps (`MAXLEN`) in this case. The last layer added is a `softmax` function `f`, as defined in the section below.

 In mathematics, the softmax function, (also called **normalized exponential function[1]**) is a generalization of the logistic function that squashes a K-dimensional vector z of arbitrary real values to a K-dimensional vector $\sigma(z)$ of real values. Each entry, after applying this function, is in the range *(0, 1)*, and also all the entries add up to 1.

4. Once the model has been built, we can see the model summary as follows:

```
Layer (type) Output Shape Param #
================================================================
lstm_1 (LSTM) (None, 128) 72192

repeat_vector_1 (RepeatVecto (None, 4, 128) 0

lstm_2 (LSTM) (None, 4, 128) 131584

time_distributed_1 (TimeDist (None, 4, 12) 1548

activation_1 (Activation) (None, 4, 12) 0
================================================================
Total params: 205,324
Trainable params: 205,324
Non-trainable params: 0
```

Model fit and prediction

1. Next, we will fit the model iteratively, as follows:

```
for iteration in range(1, 200):
    print()
    print('-' * 50)
    print('Iteration', iteration)
    model.fit(x_train, y_train,
        batch_size=BATCH_SIZE,
        epochs=1,
        validation_data=(x_val, y_val))
    for i in range(10):
        ind = np.random.randint(0, len(x_val))
        rowx, rowy = x_val[np.array([ind])], y_val[np.array([ind])]
```

```
preds = model.predict_classes(rowx, verbose=0)
q = ctable.decode(rowx[0])
correct = ctable.decode(rowy[0])
guess = ctable.decode(preds[0], calc_argmax=False)
print('Q', q[::-1] if REVERSE else q, end=' ')
print('T', correct, end=' ')
if correct == guess:
    print(colors.ok + '✓' + colors.close, end=' ')
else:
    print(colors.fail + '☒' + colors.close, end=' ')
    print(guess)
```

In the preceding code, we execute the following steps:

1. For 200 iterations, we run x_train and y_train on the model and validate the model against x_val and y_val
2. We take 10 random samples and check the predicted subtraction value and actual value

2. The preceding code gives the output, shown as follows for the first iteration:

```
--------------------------------------------------
Iteration 1
Train on 45000 samples, validate on 5000 samples
Epoch 1/1
2018-06-06 00:36:46.406357: I
tensorflow/core/platform/cpu_feature_guard.cc:140] Your CPU
supports instructions that this TensorFlow binary was not compiled
to use: AVX2 FMA

128/45000 [..............................] - ETA: 8:04 - loss:
2.4835 - acc: 0.1289
384/45000 [..............................] - ETA: 2:48 - loss:
2.4789 - acc: 0.1641
.......
44800/45000 [==============================>.] - ETA: 0s - loss:
1.8918 - acc: 0.3324
45000/45000 [==============================] - 13s 298us/step -
loss: 1.8907 - acc: 0.3327 - val_loss: 1.6774 - val_acc: 0.3900
Q 226-90 T 136 ☒ 12
Q 30-188 T -158 ☒ -322
Q 57-24 T 33 ☒ -1
Q 878-4 T 874 ☒ 833
Q 78-11 T 67 ☒ 13
Q 452-222 T 230 ☒ -22
Q 859-4 T 855 ☒ 833
Q 969-1 T 968 ☒ 833
```

```
Q 722-651 T 71 ☒ -12
Q 983-4 T 979 ☒ 833
```

 Notice all the predictions are wrong, but as we move towards the 200th iteration, the accuracy of the model increases.

3. The output listed as follows shows the output from iteration number 81:

```
----------------------------------------------
Iteration 80
Train on 45000 samples, validate on 5000 samples
Epoch 1/1
Q 208-4 T 204 ✓ 204
Q 944-826 T 118 ✓ 118
Q 484-799 T -315 ✓ -315
Q 60-408 T -348 ✓ -348
Q 94-742 T -648 ✓ -648
Q 28-453 T -425 ✓ -425
Q 173-63 T 110 ✓ 110
Q 266-81 T 185 ✓ 185
Q 819-57 T 762 ✓ 762
Q 45-904 T -859 ✓ -859
```

This recipe gives a good overview of how to do simple sequence to sequence prediction using LSTM, with an example of subtracting any two numbers.

8
Natural Language Processing Using Keras Models

In this chapter, we will cover the following recipes:

- Word embedding
- Sentiment analysis

Introduction

Why is human language so special? Human, or natural, language is a method that developed to convey meaning and is not produced by a physical action of any kind. It is quite different from vision or any other machine learning task.

Natural language processing (**NLP**) is one of the types of **Artificial Intelligence** (**AI**) that allow machines to analyze and understand the human language. NLP was begun to develop software that generates and understands natural languages so that a user can have natural conversations with his/her computer. NLP combines AI with computational linguistics and computer science to process human languages and speech.

Examples of NLP include sentiment analysis, chatbots, document classification, word clustering, machine translation, and many more. This list is long, and the scenarios in which one can use NLP are even greater in number. This chapter aims to introduce you to recipes with an understanding of NLP techniques as applied to deep learning models so that you can adapt them to your dataset with ease and develop useful applications.

Word embedding

Word embedding is an NLP technique for representing words and documents using a dense vector representation compared to the bag of word techniques, which used a large sparse vector representation. Embeddings are a class of NLP methods that aim to project the semantic meaning of words into a geometric space. This is accomplished by linking a numeric vector to each word in a dictionary so that the distance between any two vectors captures the part of the semantic relationship between the two associated words. The geometric space formed by these vectors is called an **embedding space**.

The two most popular techniques for learning word embeddings are global vectors for word representation (**GloVe**) and **word to vector** representation (**Word2vec**).

In the following sections, we will be processing sample documents through the neural network with and without the embedding layer.

Getting ready

In the first case, we will not use any pre-trained word embeddings from Keras. Keras provides an embedding layer that can be used for textual or natural language data. The input data should be numerically encoded so that each word is represented by a numerical or integer value. We can use the tokenizer API from Keras to do this. In a case where we use Keras APIs without the pre-trained embeddings, the embedding layer is initialized with random weights.

Let's first create sample documents and corresponding labels, which classify each document as positive or negative, as shown in this code snippet:

```
# define documents
documents = ['Well done!',
             'Good work',
             'Great effort',
             'nice work',
             'Excellent!',
             'Weak',
             'Poor effort!',
             'not good',
             'poor work',
             'Could have done better.']
#define class labels
labels = array([1, 1, 1, 1, 1, 0, 0, 0, 0, 0])
```

How to do it...

We will now use the Keras text processing API to one-hot encode the documents. The `one-hot` method is a representation of categorical features as binary vectors. Firstly, the categorical values are mapped to integer/numeric values. Later, the integer/numeric value is presented as a binary vector that is all zero values, except the one at the index of the integer.

We normally represent a document as a sequence of integer values, where each word in the document is represented as a single integer.

Without embeddings

Keras provides the `one_hot()` function, which you can use to tokenize and encode a text document. It does not create one-hot encoding but, instead, the function performs a `hashing_trick()` function. The hashing trick converts text into a sequence of indexes in a fixed-size hashing space:

1. Finally, the function returns an integer-encoded version of the document:

   ```
   vocab_size = 50
   encodeDocuments = [one_hot(doc, vocab_size) for doc in documents]
   print(encodeDocuments)
   ```

   The output of the preceding code is as follows:

   ```
   [[1, 39], [37, 40], [21, 19], [5, 40], [16], [36], [8, 19], [25,
   37], [8, 40], [25, 44, 39, 26]]
   ```

   Where the `Well Done!` and `Good Work` documents are represented by vectors `[1, 39]` `[37,40]` respectively. Also, you can observe how the `Could have done better` document is represented by four integers, `[25, 44, 39, 26]`.

2. We then pad the documents to a max length of four, shown as follows, because the max length of the existing vector is four integers, as seen previously. The `pad_sequences()` function in the Keras library can be used to pad variable length sequences. The default padding value is `0.0`, although this can be changed by specifying the preferred value by means of the `value` argument.

3. The padding can be used at the beginning or at the end of the sequence, described as `pre-` or `post-` sequence padding, as follows:

```
max_length = 4
paddedDocuments = pad_sequences(encodeDocuments, maxlen=max_length,
padding='post')
print(paddedDocuments)
```

The output of the preceding code is as follows:

```
[[ 1 39  0  0]
 [37 40  0  0]
 [21 19  0  0]
 [ 5 40  0  0]
 [16  0  0  0]
 [36  0  0  0]
 [ 8 19  0  0]
 [25 37  0  0]
 [ 8 40  0  0]
 [25 44 39 26]]
```

You will observe that all the documents are padded with *0* to a max length of four.

4. Now, we will create a sequential model from the Keras library, which is internally represented as a sequence of layers. First, we create a new sequential model and add layers to develop the network topology. After the model is defined, we compile it with the backend as `TensorFlow`. The backend here chooses the best way to represent the network for training and making predictions to run on the given hardware.

5. We define the embedding layer as part of network modeling, as shown in the following code snippet. The embedding has a vocabulary size of 50 and an input length of four, as defined previously. We will select an embedding space of eight dimensions. The model, in this case, is a binary classifier. Importantly, the output from the embedding layer will be four vectors of eight dimensions each, one for each word. We flatten this to one 32 element vector to pass on to the dense output layer. Finally, we can fit and evaluate the classification model.

6. We must specify the loss function to evaluate a set of weights, the optimizer used to search through different weights for the network, and any optional metrics we would like to collect and report during training. The code is as follows:

```
model = Sequential()
model.add(Embedding(vocab_size, 8, input_length=max_length))
model.add(Flatten())
model.add(Dense(1, activation='sigmoid'))
```

```
model.compile(optimizer='adam', loss='binary_crossentropy',
metrics=['acc'])
print(model.summary())
```

We use logarithmic loss, which for a given classification problem is described in Keras as `binary_crossentropy`. For optimization, the gradient descent algorithm `Adam` is utilized.

For further details on the Adam optimizer, a method for stochastic optimization, refer to `https://arxiv.org/abs/1412.6980v8`.

The output of the preceding code is as follows:

```
Layer (type)                 Output Shape              Param #
=================================================================
embedding_1 (Embedding)      (None, 4, 8)              400
_____
flatten_1 (Flatten)          (None, 32)                0
_____
dense_1 (Dense)              (None, 1)                 33
=================================================================
Total params: 433
Trainable params: 433
Non-trainable params: 0
```

Let's now fit the mode. It is time to execute the model on a given dataset or documents in this case. The training process runs on a fixed number of iterations called **epochs**. We can also set the number of instances that are evaluated before a weight update in the network is performed, called the **batch size**, and set it using the `batch_size` argument:

```
model.fit(paddedDocuments, labels, epochs=50, verbose=0)
```

7. Finally, we evaluate the performance of our neural network on the given documents. This will give us the training accuracy on the trained data itself, for now, to keep it simple. Later in the chapter, we will use training and test sets to evaluate the performance of our model. The code is as follows:

```
loss, accuracy = model.evaluate(paddedDocuments, labels, verbose=0)
print('Accuracy: %f' % (accuracy*100))
```

The output of the preceding code is as follows:

```
80.000001
```

With embeddings

In the previous recipe, we did not use any embeddings, such as **Global Vectors for Word Representation** (**GloVe**) or Word2vec; we will now use pre-trained word embeddings from Keras. Let's reuse the documents and labels from the preceding recipe. The code is as follows:

```
# define documents
 documents = ['Well done!',
              'Good work',
              'Great effort',
              'nice work',
              'Excellent!',
              'Weak',
              'Poor effort!',
              'not good',
              'poor work',
              'Could have done better.']

# define class labels
labels = array([1, 1, 1, 1, 1, 0, 0, 0, 0, 0])
```

Keras provides tokenizer APIs for preparing text that can be fit and reused to prepare multiple text documents. A tokenizer is constructed and then fit onto text documents or integer encoded text documents. Here, words are called tokens and the method of dividing the text into tokens is described as tokenization. Keras gives us the text_to_word_sequence API that can be used to split the text into a list of words as follows:

```
# use tokenizer and pad
tokenizer = Tokenizer()
tokenizer.fit_on_texts(documents)
vocab_size = len(tokenizer.word_index) + 1
encodeDocuments = tokenizer.texts_to_sequences(documents)
print(encodeDocuments)
```

The output of the preceding code is as follows:

```
[[6, 2], [3, 1], [7, 4], [8, 1], [9], [10], [5, 4], [11, 3], [5, 1], [12,
13, 2, 14]]
```

Where the Well Done! and Good Work documents are represented by vectors [6, 2] [3,1] respectively. Also, you can observe how the Could have done better document is represented by four integers, [12, 13, 2, 14].

Tokenizer text APIs from Keras are more sophisticated and preferred for production use cases over the previous approach of using one-hot encoding.

We then pad the documents to a max length of four, shown as follows; the `pad_sequences()` function in the Keras library can be used to pad variable length sequences. The default padding value is `0.0`, although this can be changed by specifying the preferred value by means of the `value` argument.

The padding can be used at the beginning or at the end of the sequence, described as `pre-` or `post-` sequence padding, as follows:

```
max_length = 4
paddedDocuments = pad_sequences(encodeDocuments, maxlen=max_length,
padding='post')
print(paddedDocuments)
```

The output of the preceding code is as follows:

```
[[ 6  2  0  0] [ 3  1  0  0] [ 7  4  0  0] [ 8  1  0  0] [ 9  0  0  0] [10
 0  0  0] [ 5  4  0  0] [11  3  0  0] [ 5  1  0  0] [12 13  2 14]]
```

We will be using preloaded GloVe embeddings, where GloVe. Basically, the GloVe method provides a suite of pre-trained word embeddings. We will be using GloVe trained with six billion words and 100 dimensions, that is, `glove.6B.100d.txt`. If we look inside the file, we can see a token (word) followed by the weights (100 numbers) on each line.

Therefore, at this step, we load the entire GloVe word embedding file into memory as a dictionary of the word-to-embedding array.

 Refer to this GloVe paper for details on GloVe: `https://nlp.stanford.edu/pubs/glove.pdf`.

The code is as follows:

```
# load glove model
inMemoryGlove = dict()
f = open('/deeplearning-keras/ch08/embeddings/glove.6B.100d.txt')
for line in f:
    values = line.split()
    word = values[0]
    coefficients = asarray(values[1:], dtype='float32')
    inMemoryGlove[word] = coefficients
f.close()
print(len(inMemoryGlove))
```

The output of the preceding code is as follows:

```
400000
```

Now, we create a matrix of one embedding for each word in the training dataset. We achieve that by iterating over all the unique words in `Tokenizer.word_index` and locating the embedding weight vector from the loaded GloVe embedding.

The output is a matrix of weights only for the words in the training set. The code is as follows:

```
# create coefficient matrix for training data
trainingToEmbeddings = zeros((vocab_size, 100))
for word, i in tokenizer.word_index.items():
    gloveVector = inMemoryGlove.get(word)
    if gloveVector is not None:
        trainingToEmbeddings[i] = gloveVector
```

As explained in the first recipe, a Keras model is a sequence of layers. We create a new sequential model and add layers to develop a network topology. After the model is defined, we compile it using `tensorflow` as the backend. The backend here chooses the best way to represent the network for training and making predictions to run on the given hardware. The code is as follows:

```
model = Sequential()
model.add(Embedding(maxFeatures, 100, weights=[trainingToEmbeddings],
input_length=max_length, trainable=False))
model.add(Flatten())
model.add(Dense(1, activation='sigmoid'))
model.compile(optimizer='adam', loss='binary_crossentropy',
metrics=['acc'])
```

We use logarithmic loss, which for a given classification problem is described in Keras as `binary_crossentropy`. For optimization, the gradient descent algorithm Adam is utilized.

The output of the preceding code is as follows:

```
Layer (type)                 Output Shape              Param #
=================================================================
embedding_1 (Embedding)      (None, 4, 100)            1500
_____
flatten_1 (Flatten)          (None, 400)               0
_____
dense_1 (Dense)              (None, 1)                 401
=================================================================
Total params: 1,901
```

```
Trainable params: 401
Non-trainable params: 1,500
```

Let's now fit the model; it is time to execute the model on the given dataset or documents in this case. The training process runs on a fixed number of iterations, called **epochs**. We can also set the number of instances that are evaluated before a weight update on the network is performed, called the **batch size**, and set using the `batch_size` argument. The code is as follows:

```
model.fit(paddedDocuments, labels, epochs=50, verbose=0)
```

Finally, we evaluate the performance of our neural network on the given documents. This will give us the training accuracy on the trained data itself, for now, to keep it simple. Later in the chapter, we will use training and test sets to evaluate the performance of our model as follows:

```
loss, accuracy = model.evaluate(paddedDocuments, labels, verbose=0)
print('Accuracy: %f' % (accuracy * 100))
```

The output of the preceding code is as follows:

```
100.000000
```

Sentiment analysis

As technology is increasing the abilities of businesses, sentiment analysis is becoming a more commonly utilized tool for various use cases. Businesses use sentiment analysis to give their users insights into how the customer feels regarding their business, products, and topics of interest.

Sentiment analysis is basically a method of computationally identifying and categorizing sentiments expressed in a piece of text or corpus in order to determine whether the composer's attitude towards a particular topic, product, and so on is positive, negative, or neutral. Sentiment analysis algorithms use NLP to classify documents as positive, neutral, or negative.

In this recipe, you will learn how to develop deep learning models for sentiment analysis, including:

- How to preprocess and load a dataset in Keras
- How to use word embeddings
- How to develop a large neural network model for sentiment analysis

Getting ready

Let's load the dataset and calculate some of its properties. We will start off by loading the sentiment dataset and extracting text and the corresponding sentiment label. We will be keeping only the necessary columns.

About this dataset

This data originally came from Crowdflower's data for everyone library (`https://www.figure-eight.com/data-for-everyone/`).

As the original source says, we looked through tens of thousands of tweets about the early August **Grand Old Party** (**GOP**) debate in Ohio and asked contributors to do both sentiment analysis and data categorization. Contributors were asked if the tweet was relevant, which candidate was mentioned, what subject was mentioned, and then what the sentiment was for a given tweet. We've removed the non-relevant messages from the uploaded dataset. The dataset is available as part of the code repository.

Next, we shall be dropping the neutral sentiments as our goal was to only differentiate between positive and negative tweets. After that, we will be filtering the tweets so only valid texts and words remain. Then, we define the number of max features as 2,000 and use a tokenizer to vectorize and convert the text into sequences so the network can deal with it as input:

```
# read input document
X = pd.read_csv('/deeplearning-keras/ch08/sentiment-
analysis/Sentiment.csv')
X = X[['text', 'sentiment']]
X = X[X.sentiment != 'Neutral']
X['text'] = X['text'].apply(lambda x: x.lower())
X['text'] = X['text'].apply((lambda x: re.sub('[^a-zA-z0-9\s]', '', x)))

for idx, row in X.iterrows():
  row[0] = row[0].replace('rt', ' ')

print(X)
```

Example text output is shown here, with columns for text and sentiment:

```
index       text            sentiment
  1 rt scottwalker didnt catch the full gopdebate ... Positive
  3 rt robgeorge that carly fiorina is trending h... Positive
  4 rt danscavino gopdebate w realdonaldtrump deli... Positive
```

```
5  rt gregabbott_tx tedcruz on my first day i wil... Positive
6  rt warriorwoman91 i liked her and was happy wh... Negative
8  deer in the headlights rt lizzwinstead ben car... Negative
9  rt nancyosborne180 last nights debate proved i... Negative
10 jgreendc realdonaldtrump in all fairness billc... Negative
11 rt waynedupreeshow just woke up to tweet this ... Positive
12 me reading my familys comments about how great... Negative
```

How to do it...

The Tokenizer API in Keras has several methods that help us to prepare text so it can be used in neural network models. We use the `fit_on_texts` method and can see the word index using the `word_index` property.

Keras provides the Tokenizer API for preparing text that can be fit and reused to prepare multiple text documents. A tokenizer is constructed and then fit on text documents or integer encoded text documents; here, words are called **tokens** and the method of dividing the text into tokens is described as **tokenization**:

1. Keras gives us the `text_to_word_sequence` API, which can be used to split the text into a list of words:

   ```
   # use tokenizer and pad
   maxFeatures = 2000
   tokenizer = Tokenizer(num_words=maxFeatures, split=' ')
   tokenizer.fit_on_texts(X['text'].values)
   # maxFeatures = len(tokenizer.word_index) + 1
   encodeDocuments = tokenizer.texts_to_sequences(X['text'].values)
   ```

   The output of the preceding code is as follows:

   ```
   [[363, 122, 1, 703, 2, 39, 58, 237, 37, 210, 6, 174, 1761, 12,
   1324, 1409, 743], [16, 284, 252, 5, 821, 102, 167, 26, 136, 6, 1,
   173, 12, 2, 233, 724, 17], so on.
   ```

2. We then pad the documents to a max length of 29, shown as follows. The `pad_sequences()` function in the Keras library can be used to pad variable length sequences. The default padding value is 0.0, although this can be changed by specifying the preferred value by means of the `value` argument.

3. The padding can be used at the beginning or at the end of the sequence, described as `pre-` or `post-`sequence padding, as follows:

```
max_length = 29
paddedDocuments = pad_sequences(encodeDocuments, maxlen=max_length,
padding='post')
```

4. Next, we will be using preloaded GloVe embeddings, as described previously in one of the recipes. Basically, the `GloVe` method provides a suite of pre-trained word embeddings. We will be using GloVe trained with six billion words and 100 dimensions, that is, `glove.6B.100d.txt`. If we look inside the file, we can see a token (word) followed by the weights (100 numbers) on each line.

5. Therefore, we load the entire GloVe word embedding file into memory as a dictionary of the word-to-embedding array:

```
# load glove model
inMemoryGlove = dict()
f = open('/deeplearning-keras/ch08/embeddings/glove.6B.100d.txt')
for line in f:
    values = line.split()
    word = values[0]
    coefficients = asarray(values[1:], dtype='float32')
    inMemoryGlove[word] = coefficients
f.close()
print(len(inMemoryGlove))
```

The output of the preceding code is as follows:

```
400000
```

6. We now convert labels to ones and zeros for corresponding positive and negative values, respectively:

```
# split data
labels = []
for i in X['sentiment']:
    if i == 'Positive':
        labels.append(1)
    else:
        labels.append(0)

labels = array(labels)
```

A learning model intends to make good predictions on the new unseen dataset. But if we are creating a model over a complete existing data set, how would we get the previously unseen data? One way is to divide the dataset into two sets, called a **training set** and **test set**, subsets of the original dataset.

7. Therefore, the dataset we use is normally split into the training set and test set. The training set contains the feature vector and corresponding output or label, which the model uses for learning in order to generalize to other datasets. We create the test dataset (or subset) in order to test our model's prediction on this subset. From scikit-learn `model_selection` sub-library, we import the `train_test_split` function to split the training and test sets as follows:

```
X_train, X_test, Y_train, Y_test =
train_test_split(paddedDocuments,labels, test_size = 0.33,
random_state = 42)
print(X_train.shape,Y_train.shape)
print(X_test.shape,Y_test.shape)
```

The output of the preceding code is as follows:

```
(7188, 29) (7188,)(3541, 29) (3541,)
```

8. Now, we create a matrix of one embedding for each word in the training dataset. We achieve that by iterating over all the unique words in `Tokenizer.word_index` and locating the embedding weight vector from the loaded GloVe embedding.

The output is a matrix of weights, but only for the words in the training set. The code is as follows:

```
# create coefficient matrix for training data
trainingToEmbeddings = zeros((maxFeatures, 100))
for word, i in tokenizer.word_index.items():
    if i < 2001:
        gloveVector = inMemoryGlove.get(word)
        if gloveVector is not None:
            trainingToEmbeddings[i] = gloveVector
```

9. As explained in the first recipe, a Keras model is a sequence of layers. We create a new sequential model and add layers to develop a network topology. After the model is defined, we compile it using `tensorflow` as the backend. The backend here chooses the best way to represent the network for training and making predictions to run on the given hardware from the following code:

```
model = Sequential()
```

```
model.add(Embedding(maxFeatures, 100,
weights=[trainingToEmbeddings], input_length=max_length,
trainable=False))
model.add(Flatten())
model.add(Dense(1, activation='sigmoid'))
model.compile(optimizer='adam', loss='binary_crossentropy',
metrics=['acc'])
print(model.summary())
```

10. We use logarithmic loss, which for a given classification problem is described in Keras as `binary_crossentropy`. For optimization, the gradient descent algorithm Adam is utilized.

The output is as follows:

```
Layer (type)                 Output Shape              Param #
=================================================================
embedding_1 (Embedding)      (None, 29, 100)           200000
_____
flatten_1 (Flatten)          (None, 2900)              0
_____
dense_1 (Dense)              (None, 1)                 2901
=================================================================
Total params: 202,901
Trainable params: 2,901
Non-trainable params: 200,000
```

11. Let's now fit the model; it is time to execute the model on the given dataset or documents in this case. The training process runs on a fixed number of iterations called **epochs**. We can also set the number of instances that are evaluated before a weight update in the network is performed, called the **batch size**, and set using the `batch_size` argument as follows:

```
batch_size = 32
model.fit(X_train, Y_train, epochs=50, batch_size=batch_size,
verbose=0)
```

12. Finally, we evaluate the performance of our neural network on the given documents. An accuracy of 81% is achieved for the sentiment analysis task with the following code:

```
loss, accuracy = model.evaluate(X_test, Y_test, verbose=0)
print('Accuracy: %f' % (accuracy * 100))
```

The output for accuracy is as follows:

```
81.191754
```

Full code listing

The full code listing is as follows:

```python
# imports from Keras and Sklearn
import csv
from numpy import array, asarray, zeros
from keras.preprocessing.text import one_hot, Tokenizer
from keras.preprocessing.sequence import pad_sequences
from keras.models import Sequential
from keras.layers import Dense, SpatialDropout1D, LSTM
from keras.layers import Flatten
from keras.layers.embeddings import Embedding
import pandas as pd
import re
from sklearn.model_selection import train_test_split


# read input document - Sentiment.csv (part of repository)
X = pd.read_csv('/deeplearning-keras/ch08/sentiment-
analysis/Sentiment.csv')
X = X[['text', 'sentiment']]
X = X[X.sentiment != 'Neutral']
X['text'] = X['text'].apply(lambda x: x.lower())
X['text'] = X['text'].apply((lambda x: re.sub('[^a-zA-z0-9\s]', '', x)))
print(X)

for idx, row in X.iterrows():
    row[0] = row[0].replace('rt', ' ')


# use tokenizer and pad_sequences for processing the input documents
maxFeatures = 2000
tokenizer = Tokenizer(num_words=maxFeatures, split=' ')
tokenizer.fit_on_texts(X['text'].values)
encodeDocuments = tokenizer.texts_to_sequences(X['text'].values)
print(encodeDocuments)

max_length = 29
paddedDocuments = pad_sequences(encodeDocuments, maxlen=max_length,
padding='post')


# load glove model 'glove.6B.100d'
inMemoryGlove = dict()
f = open('/deeplearning-keras/ch08/embeddings/glove.6B.100d.txt')
for line in f:
    values = line.split()
    word = values[0]
    coefficients = asarray(values[1:], dtype='float32')
    inMemoryGlove[word] = coefficients
```

```
f.close()
print(len(inMemoryGlove))

# convert label's Positive and Negative to 1 and 0 respectively
labels = []
for i in X['sentiment']:
    if i == 'Positive':
        labels.append(1)
    else:
        labels.append(0)

labels = array(labels)

# split data into training and testing sets
X_train, X_test, Y_train, Y_test = train_test_split(paddedDocuments,labels,
test_size = 0.33, random_state = 42)
print(X_train.shape,Y_train.shape)
print(X_test.shape,Y_test.shape)

# create coefficient matrix for training data
trainingToEmbeddings = zeros((maxFeatures, 100))
for word, i in tokenizer.word_index.items():
    if i < 2001:
        gloveVector = inMemoryGlove.get(word)
        if gloveVector is not None:
            trainingToEmbeddings[i] = gloveVector

# create sequential model and add layers
model = Sequential()
model.add(Embedding(maxFeatures, 100, weights=[trainingToEmbeddings],
input_length=max_length, trainable=False))
model.add(Flatten())
model.add(Dense(1, activation='sigmoid'))
model.compile(optimizer='adam', loss='binary_crossentropy',
metrics=['acc'])
print(model.summary())

# finally fit the model on the training dataset
batch_size = 32
model.fit(X_train, Y_train, epochs=50, batch_size=batch_size, verbose=0)

# evaluate loss and accuracy on the testing dataset
loss, accuracy = model.evaluate(X_test, Y_test, verbose=0)
print('Accuracy: %f' % (accuracy * 100))
```

Text Summarization Using Keras Models

9

In this chapter, we will cover the following recipe:

- Text summarization for reviews

Introduction

Text summarization is a method in **natural language processing** (**NLP**) of generating a short and precise summary of a reference document. Producing a summary of a large document manually is a very difficult task. Summarization of a text using machine learning techniques is still an active research topic, and references for further reading are provided at the end of the chapter. Before proceeding to discuss text summarization and how we do it, we should define what a summary is. The summary is a text output that is generated from one or more texts that conveys relevant information from the original text in a shorter form. The goal of automatic text summarization is to transform the source text into a shorter version using semantics. Lately, various approaches have been developed for automated text summarization using NLP techniques, and they have been implemented widely in various domains. Some examples include search engines creating summaries for use in previews of documents and news websites producing consolidated descriptions of news topics, usually as headlines, to help users browse.

To summarize text effectively, deep learning models need to be able to understand documents and discern and distill the important information. These methods are highly challenging and complex, particularly as the length of a document increases.

Text summarization for reviews

We will work on the problem of text summarization to create relevant summaries for product reviews about fine food sold on the world's largest e-commerce platform, Amazon. Reviews include product and user information, ratings, and a plain text review. It also includes reviews from all other Amazon categories. We develop a basic character-level **sequence-to-sequence** (**seq2seq**) model by defining an encoder-decoder **recurrent neural network** (**RNN**) architecture.

Our dataset includes the following:

- 568,454 reviews
- 256,059 users
- 74,258 products

> The dataset used in this recipe can be found at `https://www.kaggle.com/ snap/amazon-fine-food-reviews/`.

How to do it...

In this recipe, we develop a modeling pipeline and encoder-decoder architecture that try to create relevant summaries for a given set of reviews. The modeling pipelines use RNN models written using the Keras functional API. The pipelines also use various data manipulation libraries.

The encoder-decoder architecture is used as a way of building RNNs for sequence predictions. It involves two major components: an encoder and a decoder. The encoder reads the complete input sequence and encodes it into an internal representation, usually a fixed-length vector, described as the context vector. The decoder, on the other hand, reads the encoded input sequence from the encoder and generates the output sequence. Various types of encoders can be used—more commonly, bidirectional RNNs, such as LSTMs, are used.

Data processing

It is crucial that we serve the right data as input to the neural architecture for training and validation. We need to make sure that data is in a useful scale and format, and that meaningful features are included. This will lead to better and more consistent results.

We employ the following workflow for data preprocessing:

1. Load the dataset using pandas
2. Split the dataset into input and output variables for machine learning
3. Apply a preprocessing transform to the input variables
4. Summarize the data to show the change

Let's get started step by step:

1. Let's get started by importing important packages and our dataset. We use the `pandas` library to load data and review the shape of our dataset—it includes 10 features and 5 million data points:

```
import pandas as pd
import re
from nltk.corpus import stopwords
from pickle import dump, load

reviews = pd.read_csv("/deeplearning-
keras/ch09/summarization/Reviews.csv")
print(reviews.shape)
print(reviews.head())
print(reviews.isnull().sum())
```

The output will be as follows:

```
(568454, 10)Id 0
 ProductId 0
 UserId 0
 ProfileName 16
 HelpfulnessNumerator 0
 HelpfulnessDenominator 0
 Score 0
 Time 0
 Summary 27
 Text 0
```

2. Let's remove null values and unneeded features, as shown in the following snippet:

```
reviews = reviews.dropna()
reviews =
reviews.drop(['Id','ProductId','UserId','ProfileName','HelpfulnessN
umerator','HelpfulnessDenominator', 'Score','Time'], 1)
reviews = reviews.reset_index(drop=True) print(reviews.head())
for i in range(5):
    print("Review #",i+1)
    print(reviews.Summary[i])
    print(reviews.Text[i])
    print()
```

The output will be as follows:

```
Summary Text
 0 Good Quality Dog Food I have bought several of the Vitality
canned d...
 1 Not as Advertised Product arrived labeled as Jumbo Salted
Peanut...
 2 "Delight," says it all This is a confection that has been around
a fe...
 3 Cough Medicine If you are looking for the secret ingredient i...
Review # 1
Not as Advertised - Product arrived labeled as Jumbo Salted
Peanuts...the peanuts were actually small sized unsalted. Not sure
if this was an error or if the vendor intended to represent the
product as "Jumbo".
Review # 2
"Delight" says it all - This is a confection that has been around a
few centuries. It is a light, pillowy citrus gelatin with nuts - in
this case, Filberts. And it is cut into tiny squares and then
liberally coated with powdered sugar. And it is a tiny mouthful of
heaven. Not too chewy, and very flavorful. I highly recommend this
yummy treat. If you are familiar with the story of C.S. Lewis' "The
Lion, The Witch, and The Wardrobe" - this is the treat that seduces
Edmund into selling out his Brother and Sisters to the Witch.
Review # 3
Cough Medicine - If you are looking for the secret ingredient in
Robitussin I believe I have found it. I got this in addition to the
Root Beer Extract I ordered (which was good) and made some cherry
soda. The flavor is very medicinal.
```

By definition, a contraction is the combination of two words into a reduced form, with the omission of some internal letters and the use of an apostrophe.

We can get the list of `contractions` from `http://stackoverflow.com/questions/19790188/expanding-english-language-contractions-in-python`.

3. We replace `contractions` with their longer forms, as shown here:

```
contractions = {
"ain't": "am not",
"aren't": "are not",
"can't": "cannot",
"can't've": "cannot have",
"'cause": "because",
"could've": "could have",
"couldn't": "could not",
"couldn't've": "could not have",
"didn't": "did not",
"doesn't": "does not",
"don't": "do not",
"hadn't": "had not",
"hadn't've": "had not have",
"hasn't": "has not",
"haven't": "have not",
"he'd": "he would",
"he'd've": "he would have",
```

4. Clean the text documents by replacing contractions and removing stop words

```
def clean_text(text, remove_stopwords=True):
    # Convert words to lower case
    text = text.lower()

    if True:
        text = text.split()
        new_text = []
        for word in text:
            if word in contractions:
                new_text.append(contractions[word])
            else:
                new_text.append(word)
        text = " ".join(new_text)

    text = re.sub(r'https?:\/\/.*[\r\n]*', '', text,
flags=re.MULTILINE)
    text = re.sub(r'\<a href', ' ', text)
    text = re.sub(r'&amp;', '', text)
    text = re.sub(r'[_"\-;%()|+&=*%.,!?:#$@\[\]/]', ' ', text)
```

```
text = re.sub(r'<br />', ' ', text)
text = re.sub(r'\'', ' ', text)

if remove_stopwords:
    text = text.split()
    stops = set(stopwords.words("english"))
    text = [w for w in text if not w in stops]
    text = " ".join(text)

return text
```

5. We remove unwanted characters and, optionally, stop words. Also, make sure to replace the `contractions`, as shown previously. We get the list of stop words from **Natural Language Toolkit** (**NLTK**), which helps us with splitting sentences from paragraphs, splitting up words, and recognizing parts of speech. Import the toolkit using the following commands:

```
import nltk
nltk.download('stopwords')
```

6. We clean the summaries as shown in the following snippet:

```
# Clean the summaries and texts
clean_summaries = []
for summary in reviews.Summary:
    clean_summaries.append(clean_text(summary,
remove_stopwords=False))
print("Summaries are complete.")

clean_texts = []
 for text in reviews.Text:
     clean_texts.append(clean_text(text))
 print("Texts are complete.")
```

7. Finally, we save all the reviews into a `pickle` file. `pickle` serializes objects so they can be saved to a file and loaded in a program again later on:

```
stories = list()
for i, text in enumerate(clean_texts):
 stories.append({'story': text, 'highlights': clean_summaries[i]})

# save to file
dump(stories, open('/deeplearning-
keras/ch09/summarization/review_dataset.pkl', 'wb'))
```

Encoder-decoder architecture

We will develop a basic character-level seq2seq model for text summarization. We could also use a word-level model, which is quite common in the domain of text processing. For our recipe, we will use character level models. As mentioned earlier, encoder and decoder architecture is a way of creating RNNs for sequence prediction. Encoders read the entire input sequence and encode it into an internal representation, usually a fixed-length vector, named the context vector. The decoder, on the other hand, reads the encoded input sequence from the encoder and produces the output sequence.

The encoder-decoder architecture consists of two primary models: one reads the input sequence and encodes it to a fixed-length vector, and the second decodes the fixed-length vector and outputs the predicted sequence. This architecture is designed for seq2seq problems.

1. Firstly, let's define the hyperparameters such as batch size, number of epochs for training, and number of samples to train:

```
batch_size = 64
epochs = 110
latent_dim = 256
num_samples = 10000
```

2. Next, we load the `review` dataset from the `pickle` file:

```
stories = load(open('/deeplearning-
keras/ch09/summarization/review_dataset.pkl', 'rb'))
print('Loaded Stories %d' % len(stories))
print(type(stories))
```

The output will be as follows:

```
Loaded Stories 568411
```

3. We then vectorize the data:

```
input_texts = []
 target_texts = []
 input_characters = set()
 target_characters = set()
 for story in stories:
     input_text = story['story']
     for highlight in story['highlights']:
         target_text = highlight

     # We use "tab" as the "start sequence" character
     # for the targets, and "\n" as "end sequence" character.
```

```
        target_text = '\t' + target_text + '\n'
        input_texts.append(input_text)
        target_texts.append(target_text)
        for char in input_text:
            if char not in input_characters:
                input_characters.add(char)
        for char in target_text:
            if char not in target_characters:
                target_characters.add(char)


input_characters = sorted(list(input_characters))
target_characters = sorted(list(target_characters))
num_encoder_tokens = len(input_characters)
num_decoder_tokens = len(target_characters)
max_encoder_seq_length = max([len(txt) for txt in input_texts])
max_decoder_seq_length = max([len(txt) for txt in target_texts])

print('Number of samples:', len(input_texts))
print('Number of unique input tokens:', num_encoder_tokens)
print('Number of unique output tokens:', num_decoder_tokens)
print('Max sequence length for inputs:', max_encoder_seq_length)
print('Max sequence length for outputs:', max_decoder_seq_length)
```

The output will be as follows:

```
Number of samples: 568411
Number of unique input tokens: 84
Number of unique output tokens: 48
Max sequence length for inputs: 15074
Max sequence length for outputs: 5
```

4. We now create a generic function to define an encoder-decoder RNN:

```
def define_models(n_input, n_output, n_units):
    # define training encoder
    encoder_inputs = Input(shape=(None, n_input))
    encoder = LSTM(n_units, return_state=True)
    encoder_outputs, state_h, state_c = encoder(encoder_inputs)
    encoder_states = [state_h, state_c]
    # define training decoder
    decoder_inputs = Input(shape=(None, n_output))
    decoder_lstm = LSTM(n_units, return_sequences=True,
return_state=True)
    decoder_outputs, _, _ = decoder_lstm(decoder_inputs,
initial_state=encoder_states)
    decoder_dense = Dense(n_output, activation='softmax')
    decoder_outputs = decoder_dense(decoder_outputs)
```

```
    model = Model([encoder_inputs, decoder_inputs],
decoder_outputs)
    # define inference encoder
    encoder_model = Model(encoder_inputs, encoder_states)
    # define inference decoder
    decoder_state_input_h = Input(shape=(n_units,))
    decoder_state_input_c = Input(shape=(n_units,))
    decoder_states_inputs = [decoder_state_input_h,
decoder_state_input_c]
    decoder_outputs, state_h, state_c =
decoder_lstm(decoder_inputs,  initial_state=decoder_states_inputs)
    decoder_states = [state_h, state_c]
    decoder_outputs = decoder_dense(decoder_outputs)
    decoder_model = Model([decoder_inputs] + decoder_states_inputs,
[decoder_outputs] + decoder_states)
    # return all models
    return model, encoder_model, decoder_model
```

Training

1. Running the training, we use `rmsprop` optimizer and `categorical_crossentropy` as the `loss` function:

```
# Run training
 model.compile(optimizer='rmsprop',
loss='categorical_crossentropy')
 model.fit([encoder_input_data, decoder_input_data],
decoder_target_data,
          batch_size=batch_size,
          epochs=epochs,
          validation_split=0.2)
 # Save model
 model.save('/deeplearning-keras/ch09/summarization/model2.h5')
```

The output will be as follows:

```
64/800 [=>............................] - ETA: 22:05 - loss: 2.1460
128/800 [===>.........................] - ETA: 18:51 - loss:
2.1234
192/800 [======>.......................] - ETA: 16:36 - loss:
2.0878
256/800 [========>.....................] - ETA: 14:38 - loss:
2.1215
320/800 [==========>...................] - ETA: 12:47 - loss:
1.9832
384/800 [============>.................] - ETA: 11:01 - loss:
```

```
1.8665
448/800 [===============>..............] - ETA: 9:17 - loss: 1.7547
512/800 [==================>...........] - ETA: 7:35 - loss: 1.6619
576/800 [====================>.........] - ETA: 5:53 - loss: 1.5820


512/800 [==================>...........] - ETA: 7:19 - loss: 0.7519
576/800 [====================>.........] - ETA: 5:42 - loss: 0.7493
640/800 [======================>......] - ETA: 4:06 - loss: 0.7528
704/800 [=========================>....] - ETA: 2:28 - loss: 0.7553
768/800 [===========================>..] - ETA: 50s - loss: 0.7554
```

2. For inference, we use the following method:

```
# generate target given source sequence
 def predict_sequence(infenc, infdec, source, n_steps,
cardinality):
    # encode
    state = infenc.predict(source)
    # start of sequence input
    target_seq = array([0.0 for _ in
range(cardinality)]).reshape(1, 1, cardinality)
    # collect predictions
    output = list()
    for t in range(n_steps):
       # predict next char
       yhat, h, c = infdec.predict([target_seq] + state)
       # store prediction
       output.append(yhat[0,0,:])
       # update state
       state = [h, c]
       # update target sequence
       target_seq = yhat
    return array(output)
```

The output will be as follows:

```
Review(1): The coffee tasted great and was at such a good price! I
highly recommend this to everyone!
 Summary(1): great coffee
Review(2): This is the worst cheese that I have ever bought! I will
never buy it again and I hope you won't either!
 Summary(2): omg gross gross
Review(3): love individual oatmeal cups found years ago sam quit
selling sound big lots quit selling found target expensive buy
individually trilled get entire case time go anywhere need water
microwave spoon to know quaker flavor packets
 Summary(3): love it
```

See also

A Deep Reinforced Model for Abstractive Summarization: `https://arxiv.org/abs/1705.04304`

State-of-the-art abstractive summarization: `https://web.stanford.edu/class/cs224n/reports/6878681.pdf`

Taming Recurrent Neural Networks for Better Summarization: `http://www.abigailsee.com/2017/04/16/taming-rnns-for-better-summarization.html`

10
Reinforcement Learning

In this chapter, we will cover the following recipe:

- The CartPole game with Keras
- Dueling DQN to play Cartpole

Introduction

Reinforcement learning is a subset of machine learning, where AI agents learn from the environment by interacting with it and improving their performance. This branch of AI learns by trial and error instead of human supervision. The following diagram illustrates how an AI agent acts on the environment and receives feedback after each action. Feedback is made up of two parts: reward and the next state of the environment. Rewards are defined by a human:

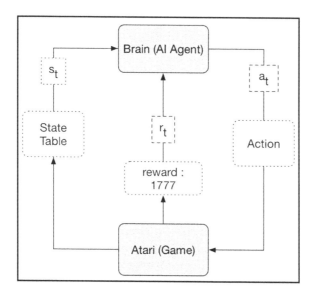

Google's DeepMind published a paper in 2013 about *Playing Atari with Deep Reinforcement Learning*. In this paper, a new algorithm called **Deep Q Network** (**DQN**). It explains how an AI agent can learn to play games by just observing the screen without any prior information about the game. The result of the experiment turned out to be pretty impressive in terms of accuracy. It opened the era of what is called **deep reinforcement learning**, a mix of deep learning and reinforcement learning.

The Q-Learning algorithm has a function called **Q function**. It is used to approximate the reward based on a state. We call it *Q(s,a)*, where *Q* is a function that calculates the expected future value from state *s* and action *a*. In the DQN algorithm, we will use a neural network to approximate the reward based on the state. In the next section, we will discuss how this works in detail.

The CartPole game with Keras

CartPole is one of the simpler environments in the OpenAI Gym (a game simulator). The goal of CartPole is to balance a pole connected with one joint on top of a moving cart. Instead of pixel information, there are two kinds of information given by the state: the angle of the pole and position of the cart. An agent can move the cart by performing a sequence of actions of 0 or 1 to the cart, pushing it left or right:

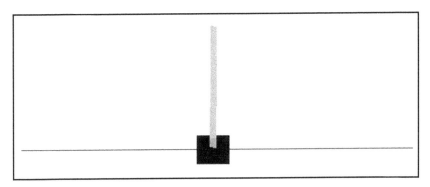

The OpenAI Gym makes interacting with the game environment really simple:

```
next_state, reward, done, info = env.step(action)
```

In the preceding code, an action can be either 0 or 1. If we pass those numbers, `env`, which is the game environment, will emit the results. The `done` variable is a Boolean value saying whether the game ended or not. The old state information is paired with `action`, `next_state`, and `reward` is the information we need for training the agent.

How to do it...

We will be using a neural network to build the AI agent that plays Cartpole. The neural network will have input with four parameters, three hidden layers, and output with two possible outputs: 0 or 1:

1. Keras makes it simple to implement a basic neural network. The following code creates an empty sequential model:

```
model = Sequential()
model.add(Dense(24, input_dim=self.state_size, activation='relu'))
model.add(Dense(24, activation='relu'))
model.add(Dense(self.action_size, activation='linear'))
model.compile(loss='mse',
              optimizer=Adam(lr=self.learning_rate))
```

We are using linear activation, **mean square error** (**MSE**) loss, and the Adam optimizer as the characteristics of the neural network.

2. For a neural net to predict based on the environment data, it has to be fed the information. The `fit()` method feeds input and output pairs to the model. The model will train on the data fed, to approximate the output based on the input.

This training process makes the neural net predict the reward value from a certain state:

```
model.fit(state, reward_value, epochs=1, verbose=0)
```

3. After training, the model now can predict the output from unseen input. When you call the `predict()` function on the model, the model will predict the reward of the current state based on the data you trained:

```
prediction = model.predict(state)
```

Implementing the DQN agent

In games, a reward is directly proportional to the score of the game. In the case of the CartPole game, if the pole is tilted right, the future reward of pushing the button toward the right will be higher than pushing it to the left; the pole will be vertical for longer. To logically represent this intuition and train it, it has to be expressed as a formula which has to be optimized. Loss is the difference between the prediction and the actual target.

The loss formula for CartPole can be shown as the following:

$$loss = (r + \gamma * max_{a'} Q(s', a') - Q(s, a))^2$$

Where:

- r: Reward
- γ: Decay rate
- s: Sequence/state
- a: Action
- a': Possible actions
- s': Probable next state
- Q: Optimal action-value function $Q(s, a)$ as the maximum expected return achievable by following any strategy, after seeing some sequence s and then taking some action a.

Keras takes care of the difficult tasks for us. We need to define our target, using a one-liner in Python:

```
target = (reward + self.gamma *
          np.amax(self.model.predict(next_state)[0]))
```

The preceding formula does the work of subtracting the target from the predicted output and squaring it. It also applies the learning rate defined while creating the neural network model. This calculation happens inside the `fit()` function. This function decreases the gap between the prediction and target by the learning rate, using gradient descent with the loss function of Adam. The approximation of the Q-value converges to the true Q-value as the program repeats the updating process. The loss decreases and the score improves and becomes more accurate.

The two most notable features of the DQN algorithm are the `remember` and `replay` methods. Both are simple concepts and are explained in the next section.

The memory and remember

One of the challenges that DQN needs to overcome is that the neural network used in the algorithm tends to forget the previous experiences as it overwrites them with new experiences. A list of previous experiences and observations is needed to retrain the model with the previous experiences. This array of experiences is called **memory** and we have use `remember()` function to append `state`, `action`, `reward`, and `next_state` to the memory.

The `memory` list in the following implementation will have this form:

```
memory = [(state, action, reward, next_state, done)...]
```

The `remember` function will store states, actions, and resulting rewards to the memory, as shown in the following snippet:

```
def remember(self, state, action, reward, next_state, done):
    self.memory.append((state, action, reward, next_state, done))
```

The replay function

A method that trains the neural network with experiences in the memory is called `replay()`:

1. First, we take some experiences from the memory and call them `minibatch`:

   ```
   minibatch = random.sample(self.memory, batch_size)
   ```

2. The preceding code will make `minibatch`: randomly sampled elements of the memories of the size, `batch_size`. The batch size is 32 for this example.

3. To make the agent perform well in the long-term, we need to take into account not only the immediate rewards but also the future rewards that we are going to get. In order to do this, we have a `discount rate` or `gamma`. This way, the agent will learn to maximize the discounted future reward based on the given state:

   ```
   def replay(self, batch_size):
       minibatch = random.sample(self.memory, batch_size)
       for state, action, reward, next_state, done in minibatch:
           target = reward
           if not done:
               target = (reward + self.gamma *
                           np.amax(self.model.predict(next_state)[0]))
           target_f = self.model.predict(state)
           target_f[0][action] = target
           self.model.fit(state, target_f, epochs=1, verbose=0)
       if self.epsilon > self.epsilon_min:
           self.epsilon *= self.epsilon_decay
   ```

The act function

The agent will randomly select an action first by a certain percentage. This is called **exploration rate** or **epsilon**. At first, the agent tries all kinds of things before it starts to learns the patterns. Subsequently, the agent will predict the reward value based on the current state and pick the action that will give the highest reward. `np.argmax()` is the function that picks the highest value between two elements in `act_values[0]`:

```
def act(self, state):
    if np.random.rand() <= self.epsilon:
        return random.randrange(self.action_size)
    act_values = self.model.predict(state)
    return np.argmax(act_values[0]) # returns action
```

`act_values[0]` looks like this: `[14.145181, 11.2012205]`. Each number represents the reward of picking action 0 and 1. The `argmax` function picks the index with the highest value. In the example of `[14.145181, 11.2012205]`, `argmax` returns 0 because the value in the 0th index is the highest.

Hyperparameters for the DQN

The following hyperparameters are passed to the DQN agent:

- `episodes`: The number of games the agent will play.
- `gamma`: Decay or discount rate, to calculate the future discounted reward.
- `epsilon`: Exploration rate. This is the rate at which an agent randomly decides its action rather than prediction.
- `epsilon_decay`: A parameter that represents a decrease in the number of explorations as it becomes better at playing games.
- `epsilon_min`: The agent should explore at least this amount.
- `learning_rate`: Determines how much the neural network learns in each iteration.

DQN agent class

The `DQNAgent` class has the following methods that embody, `model`, `remember`, and so on, which we discussed earlier:

```
class DqnAgent:
    def __init__(self, state_size, action_size):
    def _build_model(self):

    def remember(self, state, action, reward, next_state, done):
    def act(self, state):

    def replay(self, batch_size):

    def load(self, name):

    def save(self, name):
```

Each method has the following functions:

- `__init__` `(self, state_size, action_size)`: Initializes the class with `state_size` and `action_size` parameters:
  - `state_size = 4`
  - `action_size = 2`
- `_build_model(self)`: Builds the neural network model using the Keras sequential model and returns it. This model has two hidden layers with 24 neurons each. The last output layer has an output of `action_size`, which in our case is 2.
- `act(state)`: Acts based on the previous state and predicts the reward.
- `replay(self, batch_size)`: A method that trains the neural network with experiences in the memory.
- `load(self, name)`: Loads the model weights with the given name.
- `save(self, name)`: Saves the model weights with the given name:

```
class DqnAgent:
    def __init__(self, state_size, action_size):
        self.state_size = state_size
        self.action_size = action_size
        self.memory = deque(maxlen=2000)
        self.gamma = 0.95    # discount rate
        self.epsilon = 1.0  # exploration rate
        self.epsilon_min = 0.01
        self.epsilon_decay = 0.995
        self.learning_rate = 0.001
```

```
            self.model = self._build_model()

    def _build_model(self):
        # Neural Net for Deep-Q learning Model
        model = Sequential()
        model.add(Dense(24, input_dim=self.state_size,
activation='relu'))
        model.add(Dense(24, activation='relu'))
        model.add(Dense(self.action_size, activation='linear'))
        model.compile(loss='mse',
                      optimizer=Adam(lr=self.learning_rate))
        return model

    def remember(self, state, action, reward, next_state, done):
        self.memory.append((state, action, reward, next_state,
done))

    def act(self, state):
        if np.random.rand() <= self.epsilon:
            return random.randrange(self.action_size)
        act_values = self.model.predict(state)
        return np.argmax(act_values[0]) # returns action

    def replay(self, batch_size):
        minibatch = random.sample(self.memory, batch_size)
        for state, action, reward, next_state, done in minibatch:
            target = reward
            if not done:
                target = (reward + self.gamma *
np.amax(self.model.predict(next_state)[0]))
            target_f = self.model.predict(state)
            target_f[0][action] = target
            self.model.fit(state, target_f, epochs=1, verbose=0)
        if self.epsilon > self.epsilon_min:
            self.epsilon *= self.epsilon_decay

    def load(self, name):
        self.model.load_weights(name)

    def save(self, name):
        self.model.save_weights(name)
```

In the next section, we will look at how the agent created by using the preceding class is trained.

Training the agent

In this section, we look at how the agent is trained for EPISODES, improving the reward and recalculating the epsilon:

```
if __name__ == "__main__":
    env = gym.make('CartPole-v1')
    output_file = open("cartpole_v1_output.csv","w+")
    state_size = env.observation_space.shape[0]
    action_size = env.action_space.n
    agent = DqnAgent(state_size, action_size)
    # agent.load("./save/cartpole-dqn.h5")
    done = False
    batch_size = 32
    count = 0

    for e in range(EPISODES):
        state = env.reset()
        state = np.reshape(state, [1, state_size])
        for time in range(500):
            # env.render()
            action = agent.act(state)
            next_state, reward, done, _ = env.step(action)
            reward = reward if not done else -10
            next_state = np.reshape(next_state, [1, state_size])
            agent.remember(state, action, reward, next_state, done)
            state = next_state
            output = str(e) + ", " + str( time) + ", " + str(agent.epsilon)
 + "\n"
            output_file.write(output)
            output_file.flush()
            if done:
                print("episode: {}/{}, score: {}, e: {:.2}"
                        .format(e, EPISODES, time, agent.epsilon))
                break
            if len(agent.memory) > batch_size:
                agent.replay(batch_size)
        # if e % 10 == 0:
        #     agent.save("./save/cartpole-dqn.h5")
    output_file.close()
```

Having executed the sample, let's look at the `score` and `epsilon` value as a function of time:

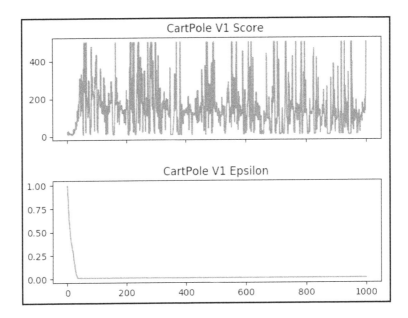

The score varies quite a bit over the period but the variations become less drastic as the agent learns how to become an expert player. Notice how the `epsilon` is also coming down drastically as it starts with a random value and then stabilizes.

Dueling DQN to play Cartpole

In this section, we will look at a modification of the original DQN network, called the **Dueling DQN network,** the network architecture. It explicitly separates the representation of state values and (state-dependent) action advantages. The dueling architecture consists of two streams that represent the value and advantage functions while sharing a common convolutional feature learning module.

The two streams are combined via an aggregating layer to produce an estimate of the state-action value function Q, as shown in the following diagram:

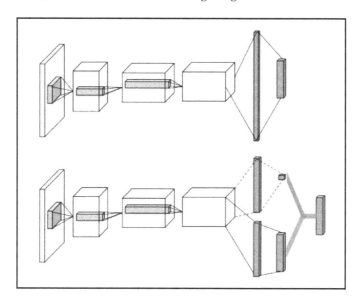

A single stream Q network (top) and the dueling Q network (bottom).

The dueling network has two streams to separately estimate the (scalar) state value (referred to as $V(...)$) and the advantages (referred to as $A(...)$) for each action; the green output module implements the following equation to combine them. Both networks output Q values for each action.

Instead of defining Q, we will be using the simple following equation:

$$Q(s, a; \theta, \alpha, \beta) = V(s; \theta, \beta) + A(s, a; \theta, \alpha)$$

A term is subtracted from the advantage function : $A(s, a; \theta, \alpha)$.

$$\frac{1}{|A|} \sum_{a'} A(s, a'; \theta, \alpha))$$

On the one hand this loses the original semantics of V and A because they are now off-target by a constant, but on the other hand it increases the stability of the optimization: with () the advantages only need to change as fast as the mean, instead of having to compensate any change to the optimal action's advantage in equation a.

Equation b:

$$Q(s, a; \theta, \alpha, \beta) = V(s; \theta, \beta) + \left(A(s, a; \theta, \alpha) - \frac{1}{|A|} \sum_{a'} A(s, a'; \theta, \alpha)\right)$$

Where,

- s: Sequence/state
- a: Action
- a': Possible actions
- s': Probable next state
- Q: Optimal action-value function $Q(s, a)$ as the maximum expected return achievable by following any strategy, after seeing some sequence s and then taking some action a
- One stream of fully-connected layers output a scalar, $V(s; \theta, \beta)$ also called **State network**
- Other stream output a $|A|$- dimensional vector $A(s, a; \theta, \alpha)$, also called **Advantage network**
- θ denotes the parameters of the convolutional layers: α and β are the parameters of the two streams of fully-connected layers

This dueling network can be understood as a single Q network with two streams that replace the popular single-stream Q network in existing algorithms, such as DQNs (DQN; Mnih et al., 2015[+]). The dueling network automatically produces separate estimates of the state value function and advantage function, without any extra supervision:

- https://www.cs.toronto.edu/~vmnih/docs/dqn.pdf
- http://proceedings.mlr.press/v48/wangf16.pdf

Now, let's look at the actual dueling network for the Cartpole game.

Getting ready

We will be using the `keras-rl` implementation of DQN (https://github.com/keras-rl/keras-rl):

```
import numpy as np
import gym
```

```
from keras.models import Sequential
from keras.layers import Dense, Activation, Flatten
from keras.optimizers import Adam

from rl.agents.dqn import DQNAgent
from rl.policy import BoltzmannQPolicy
from rl.memory import SequentialMemory
```

Let's now look at each of the three classes imported from `keras-rl`.

DQN agent

This class is already part of the `keras-rl` code base, so you don't need to implement it, but it is worth looking at what is happening behind the scenes:

```
class DQNAgent(AbstractDQNAgent):
# class methods and body
```

init method

The `init` method takes the following parameters:

- `model__`: A Keras model.
- `policy__`: A `keras-rl` policy that is defined in (policy) (https://github.com/keras-rl/keras-rl/blob/master/rl/policy.py).
- `test_policy__`: A `keras-rl` policy.
- `enable_double_dqn__`: A Boolean that enables the target network as a second network, proposed by van Hasselt et al, to decrease overfitting.
- `enable_dueling_dqn__`: A Boolean that enables the dueling architecture, proposed by Mnih et al [2].
- `dueling_type__`: If `enable_dueling_dqn` is set to `True`, a type of dueling architecture must be chosen that calculates $Q(s,a)$ from $V(s)$ and $A(s,a)$ differently. Note that `avg` is recommended in the (paper) (https://arxiv.org/abs/1511.06581).
  ```
  avg: Q(s,a;theta) = V(s;theta) + (A(s,a;theta)-
  Avg_a(A(s,a;theta)))
  max: Q(s,a;theta) = V(s;theta) + (A(s,a;theta)-
  max_a(A(s,a;theta)))
  naive: Q(s,a;theta) = V(s;theta) + A(s,a;theta).
  ```

Refer to the following papers referenced in the implementation:

- Mnih et al: `https://arxiv.org/pdf/1412.7755.pdf`
- Zing Wang: `https://arxiv.org/abs/1511.06581`

Setting the last layer of the network

The last layer of the network is chosen based on the dueling type chosen and passed to the `init` function. For example, the following code sets the output layer for the `avg` dueling type:

```
if self.dueling_type == 'avg':
                outputlayer = Lambda(lambda a: K.expand_dims(a[:, 0], -1) +
a[:, 1:] - K.mean(a[:, 1:],
                        keepdims=True), output_shape=(nb_action,))(y)
```

Dueling policy

There are various dueling policies available:

- **Eps greedy policy**: The eps greedy policy either takes a random action with the probability epsilon or takes the current best action with prob (1 - epsilon).
- **Softmax policy**: The softmax policy takes action according to the probability distribution.
- **Linear annealed policy**: The linear annealed policy computes a current threshold value and transfers it to an inner policy, which chooses the action. The threshold value follows a linear function, decreasing over time.

Init code base

The preceding described code is listed in the following snippet:

```
class DQNAgent(AbstractDQNAgent):
 def __init__(self, model, policy=None, test_policy=None,
enable_double_dqn=False,
            enable_dueling_network=False,
            dueling_type='avg', *args, **kwargs):
 super(DQNAgent, self).__init__(*args, **kwargs)

 # Validate (important) input.
 if hasattr(model.output, '__len__') and len(model.output) > 1:
        raise ValueError('Model "{}" has more than one output. DQN
expects a model that has a single output.'.format(model))
```

```
        if model.output._keras_shape != (None, self.nb_actions):
            raise ValueError('Model output "{}" has invalid shape. DQN
expects a model that has one dimension for each action, in this case
{}.'.format(model.output, self.nb_actions))

        # Parameters.
        self.enable_double_dqn = enable_double_dqn
        self.enable_dueling_network = enable_dueling_network
        self.dueling_type = dueling_type
        if self.enable_dueling_network:
            # get the second last layer of the model, abandon the last
layer
            layer = model.layers[-2]
            nb_action = model.output._keras_shape[-1]
            # layer y has a shape (nb_action+1,)
            # y[:,0] represents V(s;theta)
            # y[:,1:] represents A(s,a;theta)
            y = Dense(nb_action + 1, activation='linear')(layer.output)
            # caculate the Q(s,a;theta)
            # dueling_type == 'avg'
            # Q(s,a;theta) = V(s;theta) + (A(s,a;theta)-
Avg_a(A(s,a;theta)))
            # dueling_type == 'max'
            # Q(s,a;theta) = V(s;theta) + (A(s,a;theta)-
max_a(A(s,a;theta)))
            # dueling_type == 'naive'
            # Q(s,a;theta) = V(s;theta) + A(s,a;theta)
            if self.dueling_type == 'avg':
                outputlayer = Lambda(lambda a: K.expand_dims(a[:, 0], -1) +
a[:, 1:] - K.mean(a[:, 1:], keepdims=True), output_shape=(nb_action,))(y)
            elif self.dueling_type == 'max':
                outputlayer = Lambda(lambda a: K.expand_dims(a[:, 0], -1) +
a[:, 1:] - K.max(a[:, 1:], keepdims=True), output_shape=(nb_action,))(y)
            elif self.dueling_type == 'naive':
                outputlayer = Lambda(lambda a: K.expand_dims(a[:, 0], -1) +
a[:, 1:], output_shape=(nb_action,))(y)
            else:
                assert False, "dueling_type must be one of
{'avg','max','naive'}"

            model = Model(inputs=model.input, outputs=outputlayer)

        # Related objects.
        self.model = model
        if policy is None:
            policy = EpsGreedyQPolicy()
        if test_policy is None:
            test_policy = GreedyQPolicy()
```

```
self.policy = policy
self.test_policy = test_policy

# State.
self.reset_states()
```

BoltzmannQPolicy

In the exploration, we would like to exploit all the information present in the estimated Q values produced by our network. The Boltzmann exploration does this. Instead of always taking a random or optimal action, this approach involves choosing an action with weighted probabilities. To accomplish this, it uses a softmax over the networks estimates of value for each action. In this case, the action that the agent estimates to be the optimal one is most likely (but not guaranteed) to be chosen. The biggest advantage over the e-greedy algorithm is that information about the likely value of the other actions can also be taken into consideration. If there are four actions available to an agent, in e-greedy the three actions estimated to be non-optimal are all considered equally, but in the Boltzmann exploration, they are weighed by their relative value. With this approach, the agent can ignore actions that it estimates to be sub-optimal and give more attention to potentially promising, but not necessarily ideal actions:

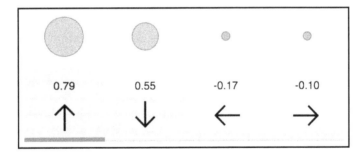

In the preceding diagram, each value corresponds to the Q value for a given action (*a*) at a random state (*s*) in an environment. The height of the light blue bars in the diagram corresponds to the probability of choosing a given action. The dark blue bar corresponds to a chosen action.

Adjustment during training

In practice, we utilize an additional temperature parameter (τ), which is annealed over time. This parameter controls the spread of the softmax distribution so that all actions are considered equally at the start of training, and actions are sparsely distributed by the end of training.

In mathematical terms, the policy can be written as shown in the following formula:

$$P_t a = \frac{\exp(\frac{q_t(a)}{\tau})}{\sum_{i=1}^{n} \frac{q_t(i)}{\tau}}$$

The following code shows how this policy is initialized:

```
class BoltzmannQPolicy(Policy):
    """Implement the Boltzmann Q Policy
    """
    def __init__(self, tau=1., clip=(-500., 500.)):
        super(BoltzmannQPolicy, self).__init__()
        self.tau = tau
        self.clip = clip
```

The Boltzmann policy is defined using the formula. In the implementation, we use it is implemented in the following snippet:

```
p = exp(Q/tau) / sum(Q[a]/tau)
```

In the next section, let's look at how these rewards, actions, and states are stored.

Sequential memory

Sequential memory is used by the DQN agent to store various states, actions, and rewards. It has the following data structures:

- **observations (dict)**: Observations returned by the environment
- **actions (int)**: Actions taken to obtain this observation
- **rewards (float)**: Rewards obtained by taking this action
- **terminals (Boolean)**: This is the state terminal:

In the code, these data structures are defined as shown in the following snippet:

```
self.actions = RingBuffer(limit)
self.rewards = RingBuffer(limit)
self.terminals = RingBuffer(limit)
self.observations = RingBuffer(limit)
```

How to do it...

Let's go ahead and implement the Dueling DQN agent-based Cartpole playing program. Perform the following steps to get the agent in place:

1. Initialize the Open AI gym environment `env`
2. Define the number of actions from `env`
3. Create a sequential neural network
4. Initialize the `SequentualMemory` with a `limit` of 100 and `window_length` of 1
5. Initialize the `BoltzmannQPolicy` instance policy
6. Create `DQNAgent`, as follows:

```
dqn = DQNAgent(model=model, nb_actions=nb_actions, memory=memory,
nb_steps_warmup=10,
               enable_dueling_network=True,
target_model_update=1e-2, policy=policy)
```

7. Compile the `DQNAgent` with the `optimization` method as Adam and the `loss` function as **mean absolute error** (**MAE**)
8. Call `dqn.fit` to find the rewards:

```
ENV_NAME = 'CartPole-v0'

# Get the environment and extract the number of actions. initiate
seed.
env = gym.make(ENV_NAME)
np.random.seed(123)
env.seed(123)
nb_actions = env.action_space.n

# A simple model regardless of the dueling architecture
# if you enable dueling network in DQN, DQN will build a dueling
network base on your model automatically

model = Sequential()
model.add(Flatten(input_shape=(1,) + env.observation_space.shape))
model.add(Dense(16))
model.add(Activation('relu'))
model.add(Dense(16))
model.add(Activation('relu'))
model.add(Dense(16))
model.add(Activation('relu'))
model.add(Dense(nb_actions, activation='linear'))
print(model.summary())
```

```
# Configure and compile the agent.
memory = SequentialMemory(limit=100, window_length=1)
policy = BoltzmannQPolicy()
# enable the dueling network
# dueling_type defined as {'max'}
dqn = DQNAgent(model=model, nb_actions=nb_actions, memory=memory,
nb_steps_warmup=10,
                enable_dueling_network=True,
target_model_update=1e-2, policy=policy)
dqn.compile(Adam(lr=1e-3), metrics=['mae'])

# now train the model
dqn.fit(env, nb_steps=1000, visualize=False, verbose=2)
```

We have modified the DQN agent to store the training `metrpet:ics` in a file. When you run it, a `log` file is generated, as shown in the following snippet:

```
20,0.46619212958547807,0.5126896699269613,-0.0582879309852918
73,0.34128815,0.47138393,0.13162555
106,0.13377163,0.5142502,0.5694133
116,0.041925266,0.5914798,0.962825
139,0.016332645,0.6163821,1.1230623
198,0.0054321177,0.7427029,1.4339473
225,0.008107586,0.8838398,1.7260511
237,0.009388918,0.9404013,1.8322802
...
1000,0.1786698,4.1688085,8.251708
```

The headers of the row are `episode`, `reward`, and `steps`.

Plotting the training and testing results

First, let's plot the training results from the saved `log` file in the `output` folder. As can be seen, the loss comes down, but toward the end escalates to an abnormal value and again comes down.

MAE and `mean_q` steadily increases as a function of episodes.

1. `mean_q` is defined by the following function:

```
def mean_q(y_true, y_pred):
    return K.mean(K.max(y_pred, axis=-1))
```

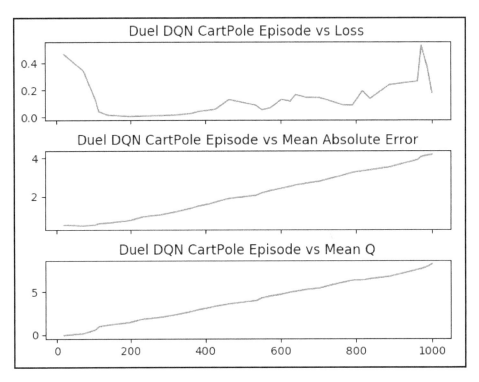

2. Let's now plot the reward and steps as a function of the episode:

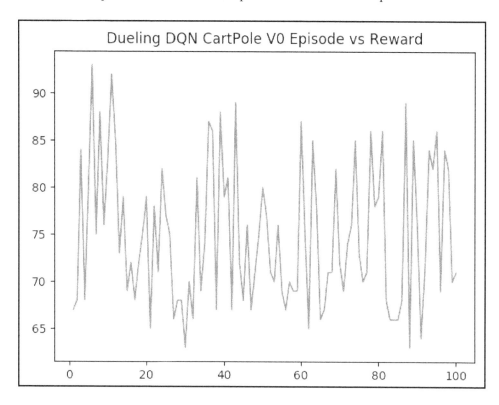

In the preceding graph, it can be seen that the reward oscillates between **65** and **95** for **100** episodes.

Other Books You May Enjoy

If you enjoyed this book, you may be interested in these other books by Packt:

Deep Learning with Keras
Antonio Gulli, Sujit Pal

ISBN: 9781787128422

- Optimize step-by-step functions on a large neural network using the Backpropagation Algorithm
- Fine-tune a neural network to improve the quality of results
- Use deep learning for image and audio processing
- Use Recursive Neural Tensor Networks (RNTNs) to outperform standard word embedding in special cases
- Identify problems for which Recurrent Neural Network (RNN) solutions are suitable
- Explore the process required to implement Autoencoders
- Evolve a deep neural network using reinforcement learning

Keras Reinforcement Learning Projects
Giuseppe Ciaburro

ISBN: 9781789342093

- Practice the Markov decision process in prediction and betting evaluations
- Implement Monte Carlo methods to forecast environment behaviors
- Explore TD learning algorithms to manage warehouse operations
- Construct a Deep Q-Network using Python and Keras to control robot movements
- Apply reinforcement concepts to build a handwritten digit recognition model using an image dataset
- Address a game theory problem using Q-Learning and OpenAI Gym

Leave a review - let other readers know what you think

Please share your thoughts on this book with others by leaving a review on the site that you bought it from. If you purchased the book from Amazon, please leave us an honest review on this book's Amazon page. This is vital so that other potential readers can see and use your unbiased opinion to make purchasing decisions, we can understand what our customers think about our products, and our authors can see your feedback on the title that they have worked with Packt to create. It will only take a few minutes of your time, but is valuable to other potential customers, our authors, and Packt. Thank you!

Index

www.ingramcontent.com/pod-product-compliance
Lightning Source LLC
Chambersburg PA
CBHW080637060326
40690CB00021B/4962